Snowbirds

The Canadian Forces Snowbirds aerobatic team pierces the air at speeds of up to 600 kilometres/hour, while performing high-precision manoeuvres such as the *Big Arrow*.

Snowbirds

**Behind the Scenes with
Canada's Air Demonstration Team**

Text and Photographs by Mike Sroka

FIFTH
HOUSE

Cover and interior design by John Luckhurst
Edited by Liesbeth Leatherbarrow
Copyedited by Geri Rowlatt
Proofread by Terry McIntyre
All official DND material contained in the book is courtesy of the
Office of Intellectual Property, Department of National Defence.

The publisher gratefully acknowledges the support of The Canada Council for the Arts and the Department of Canadian Heritage.

THE CANADA COUNCIL | LE CONSEIL DES ARTS
FOR THE ARTS | DU CANADA
SINCE 1957 | DEPUIS 1957

We acknowledge the financial support of the Government of Canada through the Book Publishing Industry Development Program (BPIDP) for our publishing activities.

Printed in Hong Kong

06 07 08 09 10 / 5 4 3 2 1

First published in the United States in 2006 by

Fitzhenry & Whiteside
121 Harvard Avenue, Suite 2
Allston, MA 02134

Library and Archives Canada Cataloguing in Publication

Sroka, Mike, 1955-
   Snowbirds : behind the scenes with Canada's air demonstration team /
   text and photographs by Mike Sroka.

ISBN-13: 978-1-894856-86-7
ISBN-10: 1-894856-86-4

1. Canada. Canadian Armed Forces. Snowbirds--
   Pictorial works. 2. Canada.
Canadian Armed Forces. Snowbirds--History. 3. Stunt flying--Canada--Biography.
I. Title.

UG635.C2S76 2006   797.5'4'0971   C2005-907208-3

Fifth House Ltd.
A Fitzhenry & Whiteside Company
1511, 1800-4 St. SW
Calgary, Alberta T2S 2S5
1-800-387-9776
www.fitzhenry.ca

Contents

Dedication

A young Miles Selby.
(COURTESY ROLAND SELBY)

This book is dedicated to the memory of Captain Miles Selby. Captain Selby tragically lost his life in a collision with Captain Chuck Mallett while practising solo manoeuvres on 10 December 2004. Flying originally as Snowbird #4 and later as Snowbird #8, his call sign was "Milhouse." Miles was a great pilot who truly enjoyed flying with the Snowbirds and connecting with young people all over North America. Always positive, Miles was more than willing to help out a photographer trying to "learn the ropes." At Comox, British Columbia, when I first met the new pilots for 2004, Miles didn't wait for me to seek him out at the base. Instead, he came over at breakfast, introduced himself, and proceeded to tell me about his father, Roland, a commercial pilot and photo enthusiast who had just seen my article on the Snowbirds in *Photo Life* magazine. After meeting Roland, the unique bond between Miles and his father was obvious. I'm not sure who was more proud of the other.

Getting to know Miles, his father, Roland, and his wife, Julie, was one of the perks of photographing the Snowbirds. Now, whenever I hear a jet flying high above and out of sight, I think of Miles. It is an honour to have known him and a privilege to say he was my friend.

Snowbird #4, Miles Selby, chats with Major Matt Beckley and Major Brian Burns of the USAF Thunderbirds prior to their ride-along.

Opposite page:
Four Snowbirds fly the *Missing Man* formation at the funeral for fallen comrade Captain Miles Selby.

Acknowledgements

I would like to thank the following people for their help in completing this book: first of all, my parents, Jerry and Joyce Sroka; my brother Jeff (and Nicole!); Adriana; Lieutenant Colonel Steve Will; Major Ian McLean; everyone at Fifth House; USAF Thunderbirds and U.S. Navy Blue Angels Public Affairs; Rob Galbraith; Bill Bishop; Anita Dammer (*Photo Life*); Simmy Chauhan (Department of National Defence Intellectual Property Advisor); Captain Mark Wuennenberg; Kevin Felker (Canon CPS); Steve Teatro (The Air Show Network); Lance Timmons; Captain Travis Brassington; Captain James Kettles; Captain Jonathan Knaul; Dan Dempsey (author, *A Tradition of Excellence*); Roland Selby; Don Pearsons; Senator Joyce Fairbairn; Clive Beddoe (WestJet); John Cudahy (International Council of Air Shows); Honorable Wilfred Moore and the crew of the *Bluenose II*; and Phil Krejcarek (the person who first handed me a camera).

Special thanks to Season Renegar at the Abbotsford Air Show.

Finally, I must thank each and every member of the 431 (Air Demonstration Squadron) Snowbirds. Without their continued support, assistance, and friendship, I would not have been able to complete this book. Cheers everyone, we finally did it!

All official DND material contained in the book is courtesy of the Office of Intellectual Property, Department of National Defence.

Foreword

The first time I saw the Snowbirds fly, I was seven years old. Watching the nine red, white, and blue jets twist and turn through their performance was thrilling. Being the aviation expert that I was, I knew that the jets were all on autopilot. Ultra-fast computers were surely controlling every movement of the formation. The pilots in the jets were probably having a fun ride, enjoying the scenery, and maybe sipping a soft drink.

Fast-forward nineteen years, to 1989. As the newly appointed Snowbird #3, Inner Left Wing, I thought back to that seven-year-old with fond memories and a smile. Having just survived the gruelling ten-day tryout process for becoming a Snowbird, two things about my seven-year-old self were very clear to me. First, watching that Snowbirds show in 1970 had significantly affected my life—here I was nineteen years later, a Snowbird. And second, that seven-year-old, self-professed expert didn't know squat about Snowbirds' flying.

The next two years would be a true learning experience for me. Like all Snowbird pilots, during the winter months I waded through endless training missions to perfect flying in formation for our shows. Exhaustive briefs and debriefs picked apart every aspect of our flying. Nothing was sacred … we all had to check our egos at the door to survive.

I was surprised at the sheer physical punishment that was involved in flying a show. Many times, I would climb out of the cockpit and discover that my middle fingers were numb from carrying so much nose-down trim. I even stopped wearing my graduation ring after slicing my finger open on it during a particularly intense practice.

Time flew by, and in the wink of an eye, we had put together the High Show, the full performance as choreographed, with all the movements included. Once we were comfortable flying overland, it was time to head to Comox, British Columbia, for two weeks of over-water training. Next it was back to our home base in Moose Jaw, Saskatchewan, to fly the Acceptance Show, which is flown in front of the commanding general for final approval, before hitting the road for six months.

My first show season was a dream come true, though it passed in a blur of transits, shows, social functions, and practices. Then, on 3 September 1989, in the skies over Lake Ontario, the unthinkable happened. My good friend and mentor Captain Shane Antaya collided with our team lead, Major Dan Dempsey, during the Upward-Downward Bomb Burst. Major Dempsey ejected safely. Shane did not.

That was the first close personal loss I had ever experienced. It was devastating. The team limped home two days after the accident, one pilot short. We spent the next week organizing a funeral and memorial service to honour our fallen comrade. Morale was low, but once we'd said our goodbyes to Shane, we regrouped and voted unanimously to complete the season. After taking a week off, we finished the remaining eight shows in Shane's honour. Then before I knew it, two years had passed in a flash.

Fast-forward eleven years, to 2002. As the newly appointed Snowbird #1, team lead, and commanding officer, I again thought about that seven-year-old and smiled. I also looked back on the twenty-six-year-old and realized that even he hadn't fully appreciated the nuances of the Snowbirds' team eleven years ago. Only as the team lead did I truly understand the effort that goes into creating and performing a Snowbirds' show. So many people put so much energy into this squadron, selflessly devoting countless extra hours to the team, from administrative support clerks to aviation technicians, from public affairs to supply personnel. And for all of them, it is a labour of love.

The Snowbirds have transcended their original role as Canada's aerial ambassadors and representatives of the Canadian military to become a truly unique symbol of what it is to be Canadian. They represent the pride and excellence found within this great country of ours. Can you imagine Canada Day without the Snowbirds flying over the Parliament buildings? Do you know anyone who does not instantly recognize the red, white, and blue colours of the Snowbirds' distinctive paint scheme and who can't then instantly identify them as "Canada's team"? Turn to page 18 in this book and see what I mean. There you'll find two unmistakable Canadian icons captured by the camera, the Snowbirds' formation in perfect symmetry with the horizon.

When Mike Sroka approached me about writing a book that would capture the essence of the entire Snowbirds' team—what it is to be a Snowbird and to be part of this group—I was intrigued, but cautious. The project was definitely an auspicious one, and although the timeline for completing the project, from beginning to end, was long, the effort seemed worthwhile.

After seeing Mike's work and listening to his impassioned sales pitch, I was sold. Mike realized that the Snowbirds' team is an intricate collage of personalities and professions and had grasped that the team is not just about the show and the pilots. *Snowbirds* embodies this notion to perfection. Mike's brilliant photos illustrate that without the concentrated effort of the entire team, the show would not go on. And, in my opinion, if the show did not go on, the seven-year-olds of this generation would miss some awesome inspiration.

Lieutenant Colonel Steve Will
Snowbird #1 (2002, 2003, 2004)

Introduction

Becoming a Snowbirds Photographer

I vividly remember three things from my youth. The first is going with my dad on opening night to see the movie *Grand Prix*, starring James Garner. The second is going to my first Indy car race, the Rex Mays Classic. The third, and perhaps most vivid, is when my dad took me to see the U.S. Navy Blue Angels Air Demonstration Team.

Although I was only ten years old when I saw the Blue Angels, the performance made such an impression on me that, in my mind, I can still see the show and the deep blue jets with the words "Blue Angels" painted in yellow. I also remember how pleased I was to get all of the pilots' autographs. It was then that I decided that the only future for me was to be a jet-fighter pilot.

Eventually my lack of perfect vision and a high school art teacher who never gave up on a student who couldn't paint or draw turned me to photography. Over the years, this has proven to be a most satisfying alternative to being a jet-fighter pilot. But looking back on what impressed me most as a youngster—car racing and aerobatics—it makes perfect sense that, as a photographer, I am also attracted to high-energy subjects such as Indy, Formula One, National Hot Rod Association drag racing, bicycle racing, and rodeo.

Many years later, in the summer of 2000, I was in Waterton National Park, Alberta, photographing wildlife, and it was time to head home. A friend suggested we go back to Calgary via Lethbridge because there was an air show taking place that weekend. We got there just in time to see the final jet demonstration, but I saw enough to decide, then and there, I'd be back the following year. I was ready for a change from photographing hotels and hospitals for corporate clients. I really missed those action-packed photo shoots.

The following summer, I went to the 2001 Lethbridge International Air Show. It was early morning as I made my way through the crowd to the "media pit." That's the photographers' area at such events that ensures we all get similar photos. I was struggling for a position at the fence when I saw the Snowbirds for the very first time. I immediately thought back to the day I had seen the Blue Angels so many years ago.

I also observed fans struggling at another fence, trying to watch the Snowbirds' team get ready. Their red, white, and blue planes were smaller and less powerful than the F-16s used by the Thunderbirds and the F/A-18s used by the Blue Angels, but impressive nonetheless. The planes were lined up perfectly and shining in the morning light. There was a flurry of activity by the blue-suited ground crew who were getting the planes ready for the performance later that day. I quickly realized the best shots would come from "over there," near the planes where the action was, not from the media pit, where I was currently positioned. So I started working out a strategy for getting "over there." Armed with a handful of impressive-looking but meaningless credentials, I managed to get access to the ramp area. After a few exposures, I noticed a red-suited, official-looking Snowbirds' officer heading straight for me. He asked, "What are you doing? You're not supposed to be here." I replied, "This is where the shots are."

Of course, I wasn't allowed to stay, but Captain Dave Sullivan did invite me to meet with him later that day. That meeting would literally change my life. "Sully" told me he was in a tryout position as public affairs officer for the team. New to the job, he was enthusiastic about raising the profile of the Snowbirds as quickly as possible. We talked about potential "joint venture" projects. What about a calendar? Trading cards?

Then I brought up the idea of a book. Sully was interested and asked me to elaborate. At the time, I didn't have much more to offer. I realized I didn't know a thing about the Snowbirds, but it seemed to me there was probably more to their story than simply the pilots and planes. So I asked Sully how many Snowbirds there are on the team, and he replied that it takes about eighty people working full time, year-round, to put the team in the air for a season. That was it—that was the story! An in-depth, behind-the-scenes look at what it takes to put the Snowbirds in the air for a full air-show season. Initially, I went to Moose Jaw, Saskatchewan, to visit the team and take some pilot portraits. A short time later, the terrorist attacks of September 11 happened, and Captain Sullivan was reassigned. The project of a lifetime seemed to end as fast as it had begun.

However, a year later, I decided to try to revive the idea of doing a book on the Snowbirds. I contacted the new commanding officer, Major Steve Will, who had just taken charge of the squadron. I arranged to meet him for breakfast at the 2002 Edmonton Air Show to discuss the possibility of resurrecting the book project. I found out later that both he and his second-in-command, Major Stu McIntosh, were there to see if my written proposal was legitimate and, if given a "green light," could actually be completed. If they decided to go ahead, I was to be given unprecedented access to the Snowbirds, access never before enjoyed by an "outsider," provided I could meet all the requirements of the Department of National Defence Office of Intellectual Property AND find a publisher committed to doing the book.

We discussed the fact I did not want to do just another jet-team book full of flying photos and little else. Instead, I wanted to take a serious look at the Snowbirds' operation "from the inside." I wanted to cover the technicians, the office staff, the home team, and, of course, the pilots. This "total coverage" of the 431 (AD) Squadron is why Major Will offered me the opportunity to do something few photographers ever have a chance to do—investigate a subject from the inside, with no restrictions. My only directive was to do what I do and do it well. I knew we would get along just fine.

The photographs in this book were taken over a four-year period, from 2001 to 2005.

Taking the Photographs

One of the secrets to shooting the Snowbirds was access—without it, I was just another photographer "behind the fence." Another secret was knowledge of the subject, without which my photographic decisions would have been based on aesthetics and little else. It also helped to have a genuine interest in the subject and to be able to give the project the time it deserved.

I eased my way into the project. It took a while for the team members to get to know me and eventually accept me into their ranks. Once they did, the nature of both the photography and the working environment changed, and they went from being "subjects" to "participants." The first year I took mostly photographs of personnel and aircraft on the ground, as I waited for the opportunity to do some serious flying with the pilots. Only by riding with them in the cockpit would I get some idea of what it is to be a Snowbird pilot. In the end, it took me six months to research the team and four years to produce the photographs for this book.

This project was an interesting ride with regard to equipment as well. Back in 2001, I was shooting Ilford and Fuji film in a pair of Canon EOS-3 cameras, but that all changed dramatically when the digital revolution hit North America. During the course of taking photographs for this book, I purchased and used the Canon D60, the Canon 10D, the Canon 20D, and the Canon EOS-1D Mark II cameras. I also learned about working in a digital environment and how to establish and manage my own digital workflow. All photos, with the exception of those from the initial Lethbridge International Air Show and the first base visit in 2001, were taken digitally.

Over the several years spent photographing for this book, I took over five thousand pictures. They were all RAW captures, shot at ISO 100 and converted to TIFF format, using Phase One software. I limited the use of Photoshop to making minor adjustments.

In the meantime, I had to adapt my high-energy photography skills to an entirely new subject matter and shooting environment. When I first arrived at 15 Wing Moose Jaw, the guard at the entrance gate said, "First left, all the way to the end." I remember all the signs saying "Restricted Area" and "No Entry" as I drove into the base. I felt like I was in another world.

At the end of the access road, I found a hangar with the word "Snowbirds" proudly displayed on its side. I was early and team personnel were just arriving. I walked into the hangar and found Major Will getting ready for the morning briefing. He said, "I see you found the place." He introduced me to the public affairs officer, Captain Stephanie Godin (now Captain Stephanie Walker), who had been instructed to show me around and familiarize me with the operation. She asked what I wanted to photograph and I simply said, "Everything."

Opposite page:
Photographer Mike Sroka "pulling Gs" during a performance flight at Comox, British Columbia.

8

As the new team members and tryout candidates went into the first briefing of the day, I was introduced to the deputy crew chief who told me I would have unlimited access to the flight line. He assigned an escort to show me where I could safely position myself to get the shots I wanted. For the next two-and-a half years I would be in the challenging and potentially dangerous environment known as the "hot ramp," an aircraft parking and taxi area that is extremely active with moving aircraft, vehicles, and crew. This meant I would have to become knowledgeable about procedures and about what was happening around me if I was going to document the show seasons properly and safely. This would become even more critical on the road where it wouldn't be only Snowbirds on the hot ramp, but other "live" military aircraft as well.

As for flying, I wouldn't be doing the typical and relatively tame media flights, but full aerobatics. It would not be easy, but I love a good challenge. Before I could even consider getting into the cockpit, I had to pass a military physical. Then came ejection seat training and parachute orientation.

I arrived at the ejection-seat trainer a few minutes before Master Corporal Mike Underwood. Mike is an expert at egress systems and responsible for training "newbies" like me to properly exit the jet in an emergency. First stop was the chute-pack room where I received a properly fitted parachute and life vest. After learning about the different chute parts and how they work, it was time to "suit up." The chute was cumbersome and heavy and made it difficult to get into the ejection-seat simulator. To tell the truth, I was a bit overwhelmed. However, I did learn how to properly get into the cockpit, and we reviewed the ejection procedures several times until it became second nature. He also reminded me that after I pulled the ejection seat "arming" pin and stowed it

Homer

People always ask me about the danger and stress involved in riding along with the Snowbirds, and I always reply that I have complete trust in their flying ability. One time I was flying with Major Chris Hope ("Homer") while the team was training over water near Comox, British Columbia. I was impressed by how relaxed Homer remained throughout the complex manoeuvres we were flying. Even as we were coming out of a major loop and heading straight for the water "at speed," he continued to discuss the flight as if we were taking a walk in the park. Meanwhile, I was definitely getting nervous as the water approached. However, without skipping a beat, Homer suddenly pulled out of the dive and, as the plane pitched hard, he calmly looked out the window and said, "Check out the whales." Just as quickly we were back in tight formation with the other Snowbirds, performing the next manoeuvre. His comfort and ability in the "driver's seat" were both evident and reassuring.

Major Hope is one hell of a pilot. So are all the other Snowbird pilots. Because of this, I had no problem whatsoever getting into the cockpit and entrusting my life to any member of this elite team.

properly, I would be sitting on a live rocket! Most people don't realize that the passenger must activate his own ejection seat. It must be so ingrained that it becomes almost pure reaction. When a situation occurs that necessitates an emergency ejection, the pilot will say, "Prepare to eject." He will then say, "Eject, eject, eject." On the third eject he is gone, and if you haven't pulled the handles you're still in the plane! And on your own! The final two stages of training are parachute orientation (where I spent a bit of time listening to MC Underwood while hanging from the ceiling) and the contract photographers' orientation flight. These flights are designed to give us a good idea of what it will be like to fly and photograph under extreme conditions.

Flying with the Snowbirds presented many challenges, both physical and photographic. Physically, the first thing I noticed was a total lack of mobility in the cockpit. I was tightly secured to the ejection seat and because the jet was a side-by-side trainer, with flight controls on both sides of the cockpit, I had to be extremely careful not to interfere with the control stick and foot pedals. The second thing that became clear to me was that the pressures exerted on the body are extreme. We didn't wear a "g-suit," which is designed to keep blood from pooling while executing aerobatic manoeuvres. To avoid blackouts, we practised forced breathing and muscle flexing. The heat and physical exertion during the flight actually result in both exhaustion and a bit of weight loss. Because photo flights were not regularly scheduled, I never really did "get used to it."

As a passenger in the cockpit, my body was always struggling to keep up with the many direction changes. As soon as my muscles flexed to fight a specific pull in one direction, the plane would pull hard in another. And just as I was getting used to climbing,
the plane would go into a dive. Or just as I was getting used to being upside down, we would flip right side up. While I was shooting pictures, I learned that if I didn't regularly take my eye out of the camera viewfinder, it could result in a case of vertigo. This could require the use of a "boarding pass," otherwise known as an airsickness bag.

Of the many photographic challenges in the cockpit, one of the biggest was keeping the digital camera from striking the instrument panel or canopy. It was also a strain to bring the camera up to my eye and keep it there. Wearing a helmet and visor presented its own challenges, but without the visor I would have ended up with a black eye from the many extreme direction changes. And last, but not least, it was important to anticipate the shots. Fortunately, because we were moving with the pack when I was shooting from the cockpit, the timing of photographs was less critical than when I was trying to catch high-speed passes shooting from the ground. If I saw the shot in the viewfinder, it was already too late.

I can honestly say nothing in my lifetime has come close to the pure elation I experienced when flying aerobatics with this team. People often compare it to a giant roller coaster. They obviously haven't flown with the Snowbirds.

My Favourite Photographs

For me, this book was all about the challenge of "telling a story" and "getting the shot." To give you an idea of what it was like to photograph the Snowbirds, I'd like to share how I "got the shot" on five of my most challenging photo ops.

1. "Over the Top"

To appreciate its full value, it's important to realize that I took this photo wearing a full flight suit, helmet, and face shield, while strapped into an ejection seat so that I could barely move. In addition, the Tutor is a light aircraft that is constantly in motion and changing direction every few seconds. Given these conditions, it's easy to understand why taking this photo was a challenge.

The idea for taking this particular photograph was to shoot at the very top of the loop and try to centre Snowbird #4 directly ahead—all this while referencing the ground and showing some of the airfield at 19 Wing Comox. I was shooting upside down, so the normal reference points didn't apply. The blood was rushing to my head as I concentrated on getting the plane ahead of us framed in the canopy glass. People often hear me say, "Photography, what a rush!" Never did it have more meaning than when I tripped the shutter for this shot.

2. "Triple Vic Takeoff" *and*
3. "The Concorde"

Capturing the pair of photos "Triple Vic Takeoff" and "The Concorde" from the end of the runway was no easy matter. I had these shots in mind from the beginning, and Deputy Commanding Officer Major Stu McIntosh helped make them happen. I needed to get permission to stand on the end of the runway, but it was worth the effort—I definitely didn't want to take these particular photos off the runway, in some field, with a super-long lens.

At the briefing that morning, I had explained what I wanted to achieve. I envisioned taking the first shot just after liftoff, with the jets flying straight at me in a Triple Vic formation. I would only get one chance to take the shot. The second photo would be even more difficult. Immediately after the Triple Vic takeoff, the squadron would re-form and fly straight at me in the Concorde formation. I wanted to be as close as possible to the jets so they would fill the frame when I tripped the shutter. Because they would be "at speed," the timing would be critical. Again, I had only one chance to get the shot.

Master Corporal Mike Underwood was my official escort on this one. We got into the crash truck and headed to the end of the runway, communicating continuously with the tower as CFB Moose Jaw is a live training facility with constant flying activity. We held position until the team was in place and ready for takeoff. Mike then proceeded to the end of the runway and we held again. Finally, I was given permission to disembark and proceed to my predetermined shooting position on the runway. Then the team was given the green light.

Through heat waves rising from the pavement, I saw the team start to roll. They were coming faster than I expected. With a 300-mm lens, I saw the first three jets leave the ground. I shot and got about eight exposures. I then grabbed a second lens without looking at the bag positioned at my feet and got only two exposures of the first three directly overhead. I remembered the Boss, Major Will, saying in the briefing, "We'll be pretty low, Mike. Be ready." A funny smile was on his face as he said it.

The noise and jet blast were crazy. The aircraft

Opposite page:
Over the Top,
above 19 Wing Comox,
British Columbia.

Camera:
Canon EOS 20D w/
Canon EF 16-35mm 2.8L

Capture:
RAW ISO 100 1/250sec@f/8

Triple Vic Takeoff, taken from the end of the runway, 15 Wing Moose Jaw, Saskatchewan.

Triple Vic Takeoff

Camera:
Canon EOS-1D Mark II w/
Canon EF 300mm IS 4.0L

Capture:
RAW ISO 100 1/750sec @ f/11

The Concorde, taken from the end of the runway, 15 Wing Moose Jaw, Saskatchewan.

The Concorde

Camera:
Canon EOS-1D Mark II w/
Canon EF 16-35 2.8L

Capture:
RAW ISO 100 1/1000 @ f/8

Two Teams – Snowbirds and United States Air Force Thunderbirds, photographed at 4 Wing Cold Lake, Alberta.

Camera:
Canon EOS-1D Mark II w/
Canon EF 16-35 2.8L

Capture:
RAW ISO 100 1/750 @ f/11

were only 15 to 18 metres (50 to 60 feet) above me. I was so surprised by how low they were, I almost forgot the second and third Vics coming toward me. I was thinking, it doesn't get any better than this. But I wasn't done yet.

I turned to see the jets flying the Concorde formation and coming straight at me, centred over the runway, flying full speed. I raised my camera, my heart pounding in my chest. In a flash they were upon me. Smoke on. I got three shots as they roared overhead. Then they turned left and headed for the Saskatoon Air Show. In a matter of minutes it was all over, but I had gotten the shots. This is what I live for.

4. "Two Teams"

The United States Air Force Thunderbirds granted me permission to visit their headquarters at Nellis Air Force Base in Nevada during the early stages of this book project. They were perfect hosts and allowed me access to the hot ramp and hangar area for several days. Because of this, I wanted to take advantage of their appearance with the Snowbirds at the Cold Lake International Air Show in Alberta to shoot a photograph of the two teams together. As I sat at lunch one day wondering how to go about this, one of the Snowbird coordinators came over to tell me that the Boss, Major Will, would like me to try to get a shot of the two teams together. Talk about being on the same wavelength! The first consideration was when to do it. The second was where.

Because of light angles, team commitments, and other factors, we decided to shoot about an hour after the final show. Where to shoot this photo proved to be a bit tougher to decide. After consulting with the Thunderbirds, we decided on a ramp "intersection" between the two areas where the teams were parked. This would provide room to manoeuvre the planes

and to pose all the personnel. I also needed a high vantage point from which to take the shot. We eventually found a ladder used to load aircraft, and a plane from each team was moved into position.

As we started to assemble people, one of our techs ran up the ladder to tell me that show officials had just told him we could not shoot here after all. When I asked why, he simply pointed behind me. The air show had been over for an hour and we hadn't realized this part of the airfield had been reactivated. There was now a WestJet 737 and several other commercial aircraft waiting to taxi through "our" intersection.

You never saw such activity by two professional ground crews to move equipment. I watched two Snowbirds' technicians towing Snowbird #1, and I could see it wasn't as easy for the Thunderbirds. A tow vehicle and proper tow bar were not available. To their credit, they came up to me and asked where I wanted the plane. I pointed to the end of their flight line. Ever try to push an F-16 with bare hands? It's not easy and it was quite a distance, but the Thunderbirds' crew chief simply said to his team, "Make it happen." And they did. Not one complaint. Even a few pilots helped. The resulting photograph—"Two Teams"—was worth the effort.

And just to show how things come back when you least expect them, later in the season, WestJet hosted the Snowbirds at an employee barbecue held at the airline's headquarters in Calgary, Alberta. As I exited their flight simulator, one of the WestJet employees asked if I was the guy on the ladder in Cold Lake who had delayed their takeoff? I said yes and when I apologized, he replied, "No need to apologize. All the passengers thought it was quite interesting to watch!" He wondered how the shot had turned out. Here it is.

Two Canadian Icons, off the coast of Nova Scotia.

Camera:
Canon EOS-1D Mark II w/
Canon EF 28-70 2.8L

Capture:
RAW ISO 100 1/1000 @ f/11

About the *Bluenose II*

The *Bluenose II,* Nova Scotia's sailing ambassador, calls the port of Lunenburg home. She is an identical replica of the famous schooner *Bluenose* (1921–46), designed by William J. Roué and featured on the Canadian dime since 1937. The original *Bluenose* raced for eighteen years and was never defeated.

The *Bluenose II* is 43.5 metres (143 feet) long and was launched from the Lunenburg shipyard of Smith and Rhuland in July 1963. She is the symbol of Nova Scotia around the world, representing excellence in ship design, shipbuilding, and seamanship.

For more information, contact the *Bluenose II* Preservation Trust in Lunenburg, Nova Scotia, or visit the *Bluenose II* website (http://www.bluenose2.ns.ca). (*Bluenose II* © Bluenose II Preservation Trust)

5. "Two Canadian Icons"

Taking this photo turned out to be a career-defining moment for me, and yet most people looking at it would never know what was involved. "Two Canadian Icons" is one of those photos where everything came together so well you can't tell the photo was taken from a moving aircraft. But, of course, that wasn't the case. Not even close!

First, some background. One day in Toronto we were talking about a potential photo shoot in Halifax that would feature the Snowbirds in flight against a maritime backdrop. We considered several ideas for the background, including ocean, coastline, warships, and Peggy's Cove. Then Captain Lyle Holbrook suggested including the *Bluenose II* as part of the setting. He offered to look into it and to get back to me if it proved "doable." I was excited by the prospect of shooting the Snowbirds with the *Bluenose II,* but I had no idea of what I was getting into. It was while we were having coffee after the Halifax air show that Lyle informed me that the Snowbirds-*Bluenose II* shoot was a go.

A few minutes later, I was told that Major Ian McLean would be my pilot. Fresh out of CF-18s, he and Major Will had put something together. That's when I saw another one of those smiles. If these guys weren't so good, I would have been nervous. Okay, I was still a bit nervous. But my confidence in the ability of these pilots to take me to the edge, allow me to get the shots, and return safely to the field never wavered. They are the epitome of the word "professional."

On the day of the photo shoot, we had our pre-flight briefing, taxied out the runway, and were soon in the air. After a beautiful ride down the Nova Scotia coast, we turned out to sea and, before long, saw the *Bluenose II* under sail. She was truly magnificent. Major McLean (call sign "Manic") and I split off from the main formation and positioned ourselves for the photo run, dropping out of the sky and levelling out at a safe distance "above the deck." At the same time, Major Will (call sign "Swill") took the nine planes into a Line Abreast formation. Major McLean informed me that we would coordinate with Major Will to ensure that everyone arrived over the *Bluenose II* at precisely the same moment.

Major McLean tapped on my shoulder and pointed to the *Bluenose II,* which was small but getting larger much faster than I ever expected. We were moving at an incredible speed. I scanned the horizon for lights. Everything was happening crazy fast and, as always, my heart was pumping out of my chest. Major McLean's voice came across the radio: "Lights at 11:00." I responded, "Got 'em." Before I knew it, we were pulling up over the *Bluenose II* and the Snowbirds flashed by, just to the right. We pulled hard and I felt incredible compression. My helmet tapped the canopy as we pulled up to the right. "Did you get it?" Manic asked. "Not even close," I replied.

We all regrouped and tried it again. This time I was ready. I picked up the formation. As we got close to the *Bluenose II* I realized, as did Manic, that we were there too soon and that the formation was a bit late. We broke off "the attack" and Manic said, "My fault, sorry. We have just enough fuel for one more pass. You okay for one last try?"

My stomach was getting a bit queasy from travelling at such high speeds with all the direction changes. It was all happening so fast that I couldn't get my eye out of the viewfinder. This compounded the problem. As I'd already learned, if you don't take your eye out of the viewfinder once in a while when you're flying, it seriously affects your sense of orientation. But, without thinking, I replied, "Go for it!" As we came around for the last high-speed pass, I thought to myself, "This is it. All or nothing. We've committed a lot of resources to this thing. It's not cheap to send up the squadron. And we have the *Bluenose II* out as well! What do I tell everyone at the debriefing if I don't come back with something?"

I have taken well over a million exposures in my career, but after twenty plus years, it had come down to one photo. No pressure. Yeah, right! Suddenly, Manic was saying, "Birds at 11:00!" I saw their headlights and replied, "I see them!" I was concentrating so hard that I was not aware of the water going by at a thousand miles an hour! Okay, maybe not that fast, but it sure felt like it. I was aware that we were pitching a bit as Manic controlled the high-speed approach. He timed it beautifully and so did Major Will. We all arrived at the same moment, and I got off four exposures before we pulled up hard. Almost immediately, Major Will asked Manic, "Did he get it?" I looked down at my camera and smiled. Although I hadn't said anything, I heard Manic reply, "Affirmative."

The Snowbirds' Contract Photographers

One group that is essential for getting the Snowbirds' message out to the general public is that of the Snowbirds' contract photographers. These talented photographers—Rafe Tomsett, Bob McIntyre, Garry Cotter, Bob Granley, Rick Radell, Ken Lin, and Janet Trost—are charged with documenting each Snowbirds season. They deliver still photography and video to the team to support the official website and various printed materials.

The Snowbirds' logo graces the floor of
Hangar 6 at 15 Wing Moose Jaw, Saskatchewan.

The Birth of a Canadian Icon

Since their inception, the Snowbirds' mission has been constant: "To demonstrate to the North American public the skill, professionalism, and teamwork of the men and women of the Canadian Forces. As the Snowbirds strive for perfection in formation aerobatic flight, they draw upon the spirit and example of those who have served before them."

Canadian military formation-aerobatic teams have played a distinguished role in our military aviation history. Since the launch of the Siskins in the 1930s, there have been many teams, all of whom have exemplified the skill and proficiency common to our Air Force pilots and ground crew. The Golden Hawks and the Golden Centennaires are still remembered by many people who enjoyed their exciting aerobatic displays. Today, the Canadian Forces Snowbirds are honoured to carry on the fine traditions established by their forerunners.

Colonel O. B. Philp, former commanding officer of the Centennaires and base commander of Canadian Forces Base Moose Jaw (now 15 Wing Moose Jaw), established the original Snowbirds' team in 1971. It was comprised of volunteer instructor pilots from the Canadian Forces Flying Training School in Moose Jaw, Saskatchewan. They flew seven ex-Centennaire Tutor aircraft, practising in the evenings and performing on weekends.

The new team was named "Snowbirds," the result of a name-the-team contest held at the base elementary school in June 1971. The winning entry was submitted by Doug Farmer, a Grade 6 student. The team first appeared as the Snowbirds at the Saskatchewan Homecoming Air Show in 1971. This performance was followed by appearances at other major air shows and at military bases across Canada. During their first show season, the team performed twenty-seven times. Public response indicated that re-establishing a Canadian formation team was a popular move.

In September 1977, the Snowbirds, who had

operated on a year-to-year basis for seven years, were made a permanent unit, and their official designation became the Canadian Forces Air Demonstration Team. Then, on 1 April 1978, the team received squadron status and became the 431 (Air Demonstration) Squadron. Its namesake, the 431 "Iroquois" Squadron (with its motto "The Hatiten Ronteriios" or "Warriors of the Air"), was a World War II bomber squadron that was disbanded in 1945. It was re-formed briefly in 1954 as an F-86 Sabre squadron and contributed four aircraft to the "Prairie Pacific" aerobatic teams.

The 431 (Air Demonstration) Squadron's crest also originates with its namesake, depicting the 431 "Iroquois" Squadron Warriors of the Air. The more familiar red-and-white Snowbirds' logo has a completely different origin, however. The design, created by D. V. Berger-North ("Badger"), was inspired by a

graphic on a matchbook. It displays four speed birds flying in formation and resembles an ear of wheat, in honour of wheat-growing Saskatchewan, the team's home province. The same speed bird appears on the bottom of each of the Snowbirds' aircraft.

The Snowbirds are goodwill ambassadors for two organizations: CHILD (http://www.child.ca/), which advocates for children with intestinal and liver disorders, and SMARTRISK (http://www.smartrisk.ca/), which helps people see the risks in their everyday lives and shows them how to take those risks in the smartest way possible so they can enjoy life to the fullest. The Snowbirds provide greater awareness of these organizations and their goals through activities such as public appearances and air demonstrations.

A Brief Overview of the Team's History

Year	Highlights

1971

- Team lead: Major Glen Younghusband
- Starts flying as an unofficial, non-aerobatic team in Moose Jaw, Saskatchewan; comprised of volunteer instructor pilots and ground crew
- Flies seven CT-114 Tutor jets and performs in twenty-seven air shows in first season

1972

- Team lead: Major Glen Younghusband
- Team adds two solo aircraft
- Flies twenty-five shows in second season

1973

- Team lead: Major George Miller
- Show expands to include aerobatic formation manoeuvres; formation changes are prohibited
- Flies first air shows in the United States
- Pilots begin wearing distinctive red flying suits that become a Snowbirds' trademark

1974

- Team lead: Major George Miller
- Cleared to perform a fully aerobatic formation display
- Aircraft repainted in the distinctive red, white, and blue scheme that is still used today
- First spring training session held at Comox, British Columbia; this becomes an annual affair
- After performing at Inuvik, NWT, becomes the first North American formation team to fly a show north of the Arctic Circle
- Performs in eighty shows for two million viewers

1975

- Team lead: Major Denis Gauthier
- Made separate but not permanent unit of the Canadian Forces
- Performs at midnight on 11 May in Inuvik, NWT, the "land of the midnight sun"

1976

- Team lead: Major Denis Gauthier
- Popularity grows in the United States and team performs in Philadelphia on 4 July as part of American bicentennial celebrations
- Performs at Montreal and Kingston as part of the Summer Olympics' ceremonies

1977 and 1978

- Team lead: Major Gord Wallis
- Becomes permanent unit of the Canadian Forces in September 1977

- On 1 April 1978, receives squadron status and is named 431 (Air Demonstration) Squadron, after a World War II bomber squadron known as The Hatiten Ronteriios or Warriors of the Air

1979 and 1980

- Team lead: Major Tom Griffis
- Performance expands into a nine-plane show, which is very popular; today, only three teams in the world fly nine-plane formations
- Performs for more than five million spectators

1981 and 1982

- Team lead: Major Mike Murphy
- For the first time, show opens and closes with nine-plane formation sequences
- Performs for more than six million spectators in 1982

1983 and 1984

- Team lead: Major George Hawey
- In 1984, helps celebrate 75th anniversary of powered flight in Canada and 60th anniversary of the Royal Canadian Air Force
- Performs in 133 shows over the two-year period

1985 and 1986

- Team lead: Major D. F. Huyghebaert
- On 9 August 1986, participates in historic five-plane fly-past, consisting of one aircraft from each of the different military demonstration teams from Europe and North and South America
- Performs in 121 shows throughout North America over the two-year period

1987 and 1988

- Team lead: Major Dave Wilson / Major Denis Beselt (1987); Major Denis Beselt (1988)
- In 1988, performs at opening ceremonies of Winter Olympics in Calgary, Alberta
- Performance seen by almost two billion people around the world

1989 and 1990

- Team lead: Major Dan Dempsey
- 1990 is 20th anniversary season
- During 1990, flies 1,000th official air demonstration and incorporates use of red and white smoke at several major show sites

1991 and 1992

- Team lead: Major Bob Stephan
- Performs briefly with U.S. Navy Blue Angels during Walt Disney World's 20th anniversary celebrations in fall of 1991
- Performs in opening ceremonies of 1991 Grey Cup game

- In 1992, performs for Inuit Circumpolar Conference at Inuvik, NWT, and as official ambassadors for Canada's 125th birthday celebrations
- Performs in 125 shows over the two-year period

1993 and 1994

- Team lead: Major Dean Rainkie
- In 1993, gives first performances outside Canada and the United States with three aerial demonstrations in Guadalajara, Mexico
- Also commemorates 70th anniversary of Royal Canadian Air Force by proudly displaying a tribute to the RCAF on each aircraft
- Performs in sixty-four shows before an estimated 3.6 million spectators in 1994

1995 and 1996

- Team lead: Major Steve Hill
- 25th anniversary of 431 (Air Demonstration) Squadron; founding father of the team, Colonel O. B. Philp, passes away early in 1995 and the 1995 season is dedicated to his memory
- Performs in 145 shows throughout Canada and the United States over the two-year period

1997 and 1998

- Team lead: Major Darryl Shyiak
- In 1998, Major Shyiak dedicates a new manoeuvre called the Philp Roll to the father of the Snowbirds, Colonel O. B. Philp
- Performs in 130 shows before an estimated four million spectators over the two-year period
- During previous twenty-eight seasons, the team has performed in more than 1,575 shows before more than eighty-five million spectators

1999, 2000, and 2001

- Team lead: Major Bob Painchaud
- Performs in more than ninety shows in over seventy locations across North America in 2000

2002, 2003, and 2004

- Team lead: Major Steve Will
- Performs in sixty-five shows in over forty-one locations across North America in 2004

2005

- Team lead: Major Ian McLean
- 35th anniversary of the Snowbirds
- Performs in 60 shows across North America in 2005

The Show Team

The 431 (Air Demonstration) Squadron consists of approximately eighty Canadian Forces personnel, twenty-four of whom comprise the show team that travels during the show season. The show team has eleven aircraft: nine for aerobatic performances, including two solo aircraft, and two spares flown by the team coordinators—the "advance" team.

In addition to the pilots and team coordinators, a number of others round out the ranks of the show team: the crew chief and deputy crew chief; the lead avionics technician; the lead aviation technician; the public affairs officer; the squadron standards and training officer; and a group of invaluable show technicians who are dedicated to "keeping the show in the air."

Due to budget restraints, the limited range of their aircraft, and to allow rotation of technicians, the Snowbirds do not simply stay on the road for the full season. Instead, the season is divided into "swings," or clusters of shows that can be done in concentrated areas. Between each swing the team returns to Moose Jaw. Each show season consists of approximately five swings. Four technicians—the crew chief, the deputy crew chief, the lead avionics technician, and the lead aviation technician—travel with the team for the complete season, working every air show. The rest of the road team changes with each swing. This allows all technicians the ability to work in an air show environment and experience "being on the road."

The Boss

The pilot who leads the squadron, both on the ground and in the air, goes by many names. Officially, he is the squadron commander. He is also known as the team lead. To his pilots and crew, he is known simply as "Boss."

When it comes time to select a new boss, the current boss puts names forward to the wing commander and the commanding general of 1 Canadian Air Division. Candidates must have served previously with the Snowbirds and hold the rank of major. The commanding general then offers the position to the pilot felt best suited to handle the demands of the job.

The job isn't an easy one. The boss' duties and responsibilities are many. First and foremost, he is the commanding officer of a Canadian Forces squadron. In this position, he looks after all members of the team. He manages the day-to-day activities of the eighty or so full-time personnel in the squadron, as well as each individual's career path. The boss is also charged with caring for the unit's resources, which include approximately twenty aircraft, several hangars, and a variety of tools. All squadron maintenance is done in-house and is a year-round concern.

The commander of the Snowbirds is also the lead pilot. Everyday, as team lead, he flies as Snowbird #1 in the very challenging and dynamic environment of low-level formation aerobatics. This type of flying is demanding, both physically and mentally, so the team lead must measure up to the task.

Finally, the boss interacts with the public and the chain of command outside the unit. The Snowbirds are part of the public relations plan for the entire Canadian Armed Forces. As the leader of the Snowbirds, the boss strives to make customers in the air-show business happy with their "product," all the while advancing the cause of recruiting individuals for the Canadian Armed Forces.

The Pilots

Snowbird pilots are exceptionally skilled individuals for whom high-precision flying is second nature. A full tour for them is usually three years. Every year the team tries to rotate one third of its members, which allows for overlap and the opportunity to always have experienced pilots training the newcomers. Incoming pilots have varying backgrounds, including flight training, CF-18 fighter squadrons, and helicopters.

Applications are filed in August by pilots whose names are put forward by commanding officers from all areas of the Canadian Air Force. During tryouts at the Snowbirds' home base in Moose Jaw, Saskatchewan, the candidates are evaluated by current team members. Major Ian McLean explained the philosophy behind the selection process this way:

> Pilots who apply for the team must have a minimum of 1,300 hours military jet time. We check on individuals with other pilots we know, asking questions about personality, work ethic, public relations skills, and social behaviour. The Snowbirds function as a very tightly knit unit and we are on the road working together for a good portion of the year. For this reason, it is important that we have individuals

who can fulfill their duties with the public but equally important is their ability to work in the team environment and get along with everyone else. If they have these qualities and are selected for a tryout, we then choose the pilots that demonstrate the best aptitude for Snowbirds' flying. The tryouts themselves are gruelling and demand a lot, both physically and emotionally, from the individuals trying out. Our system appears to work as we consistently get top performing, very capable individuals on the team.

The number of applicants applying to the Snowbirds varies from year to year. The process is designed to get the final selection down to two tryout pilots for each available position. At the beginning of tryouts, candidates attend a welcoming orientation during which they learn what is expected of them through a series of presentations, handouts, and discussions. Then, bright and early Monday morning, the "new guys" arrive at the hangar. You can feel the excitement in the air. You can also sense the tension.

Initially, candidates are evaluated for their "natural flying ability." The tryout pilots are tested on basic formation skills, flying with up to four aircraft. As for aerobatics, they are limited to individual flights that involve only basic manoeuvres. During the tryout period, the candidates fly with various veteran pilots, who watch to see if they exhibit specific skills that are suitable for particular positions. They fly two "hops" each day. After each hop, the candidates write up a self-evaluation of that particular flight. A candidate's ability to self-evaluate is an important part of the initial assessment. As I witnessed throughout the season, each air show debrief has the pilots going through this same sort of self-evaluation. Although it may look flawless to the air show audience, there is no such thing as a "perfect" performance. Constant evaluations and adjustments are a daily part of the air show season. The candidates learn this very early on during their debriefings. I had the privilege of sitting in on several debriefings during tryouts, and some got quite intense. It is critical that any and all mistakes are recognized and addressed. The partnered Snowbird also writes an evaluation and discusses the flight with his tryout pilot. Candidates are also evaluated in terms of their ability to interact with other team members, the public, and the media. Regardless of their background, whether it is flying Harvard trainers, CF-18s, or Sea-King helicopters, all pilots find the tryout experience quite intense. Each day, it's fly, evaluate, fly again, evaluate again.

The day of reckoning usually arrives on Thursday of the second week of tryouts. After one last set of evaluation flights in the morning, it's time for the long meeting in the briefing room. Only Snowbirds are present, and the discussion of who will be next to join the Snowbirds' team takes place behind closed doors. It isn't easy to reach a decision—each pilot has to be an exceptional aviator just to be nominated and then to make it to the final tryouts. Eventually, each candidate is summoned by the commanding officer and told whether or not he or she has made the team. When the official announcements are made later in the day, everyone celebrates and then rests. Training begins Monday.

During training, the pilots' flying skills are honed, first in the area of solo and group flying, then in formation aerobatics. The initial practice formations are quite loose, but with time they tighten. Eventually, they tighten even more. One pilot explained how he thought he had gotten as tight as he could in a particular formation when the veteran Snowbird in the other seat instructed: "Half again."

Pilots train twice a day, five days a week, for

several months. During this time they get more comfortable with the aircraft, with tight-formation flying, and eventually with the actual show, called the High Show, planned for the upcoming season.

When April rolls around, it is time to deploy for training to 19 Wing Comox on Vancouver Island—the team's home-away-from-home for at least two weeks every year. The team, both veterans and new members alike, have spent months training in Moose Jaw. They move the training operation to Comox to fine-tune the show in a different environment. The prairie terrain around Moose Jaw is typically flat and the weather consistently good at that time of year. Training at Comox gives the Snowbirds the opportunity to practise over water and mountains in more variable weather. This is where they become "of a single mind."

Before the team can officially hit the road for another air show season, the new show must be performed for the commanding general of 1 Canadian Air Division. This is known as the Acceptance Show. After observing the performance, the general signs the papers authorizing the deployment of the 431 (Air Demonstration) Squadron for the current season. There has been only one occasion when the general withheld his signature until "a few adjustments" had been made to the performance.

Friends, family, and other loyal supporters come out to watch the show and see what changes have been made to the previous year's performance. Then there is a celebration dinner, and soon it's time to go "on the road."

Reflections on Photographing at 19 Wing Comox

When I first arrived at Comox, I found the air base quietly hidden away next to the waters of the Strait of Georgia, with a view of the Beaufort Mountains to the west and the mountains of the British Columbia mainland across the strait. Not a bad setting for photographing Snowbirds!

The first day I positioned myself with the team coordinators down at the water's edge. Eagles were flying overhead and the day was pleasant. Quite warm, in fact. As we set up in this secluded area, several locals began to arrive in anticipation of the day's first show practice. The coordinators performed a sound check and told the crowd they were happy to be back in Comox. Everyone applauded, and within a few minutes we heard the voice of Captain Gavin Crouch: "Good morning, ladies and gentlemen ..." And so began the first Snowbirds' practice show of the day. Seconds later, the Snowbirds' team, in a Reverse Wedge formation, roared over the crowd from behind and headed out over the water. Everyone cheered, dazzled by a spectacular Snowbirds' performance over the water. All this and snow-capped mountains providing a majestic backdrop!

That day, I noticed a few planes out of position on the burst. And, the solo cross was stage right. Over the next several days, these items were sorted out and it wasn't long before we saw perfect timing and spacing in the formations. It was impressive.

Precision and pride are the two words that have come to define the Snowbirds for me. As we all said goodbye to Comox and headed back to Moose Jaw, the team was finally ready for the new show season.

The Coordinators

Most people know the coordinators as the two "red suits" who narrate the Snowbird's show. But their duties involve much more than simple narration! Snowbirds 10 and 11 are also responsible for creating the team's show schedule each year, which is no small task. I asked Captain Gavin Crouch to provide me with a few words regarding how the team decides which air shows they will fly each year. This was his response:

> Our proposed schedule for the coming season is announced at the ICAS (International Council of Air Shows) convention [held every November]. I say proposed because it does not get approved by Ottawa until early in the new year.
>
> The scheduling process for us is several months of piecing together requests from all over North America. The deadline for requests is September of the preceding year. This gives us almost two months to plan. It sounds like a lot of time but we are still on the road.... We generally get about three times as many requests for shows as we have open show dates. Some are easily taken out of the running due to their location and inflexibility for show dates. Once the schedule is complete, we brief the Commander of 1 Canadian Air Division in Winnipeg and then the Chief of the Air Staff in Ottawa.

And it doesn't slow down after the show schedule is approved. Captain Crouch explained that after Christmas the coordinators begin a series of pre-siting winter visits, which allow them to sit down with each of the individual show site representatives and get a feel for what each show will be like. They also are continually answering a barrage of emails and phone calls from the selected show sites, which prompted Crouch to remark, "it is often joked that the coordinators have cell phones permanently attached to their ears."

If that wasn't enough, they are also the "behind the scenes" and "go to" guys at each air show. The coordinators arrive two hours ahead of the team and make sure the proper number of hotel rooms and rental cas are available. They also confirm such details as show and practice times, security, points of contact, autograph locations, timings and dress for social functions, servicing requirements, laundry, gym, internet access, and VIP access for family and friends.

Each show has a primary coordinator. The other coordinator assists him. Upon arrival at the show site, the coordinators will debrief their flight, then go over operational requirements for the arrival of the rest of the team. They will decide on an appropriate parking

About the Show Team Operations Officer

"I'm the operations officer for the show team, so it's my responsibility to liaise with the crew chief in matters regarding aircraft maintenance and serviceability. It's also my job to worry about the security of our aircraft when we're on the road. I've spent a lot of time watching weather reports and forecasts, because it would only take one serious hailstorm while the team members are relaxing at the hotel to damage enough airplanes to prematurely end an entire season!"—*Captain Chuck Mallett*

plan for the aircraft, assign the vehicles to the team and confirm delivery of fuel, diesel, and oxygen for the jets. The primary, or "lead" coordinator, will have a last-minute meeting with the show organizers to confirm all is in order, then fill out the "over wing" briefing sheet. The "over wing" briefing ensures the team is all on the same page and takes place when the rest of the squadron arrives. It always occurs over the wing of the number 5 jet, as this aircraft is parked in the middle of all the others.

For the performances, the coordinators attend both the briefings and debriefings. During the briefing it is decided which standard portions of the show will be dedicated to local individuals or groups. During the show, the coordinators confirm restricted airspace is active and get takeoff and taxi clearance for the team. They are the only point of contact between the Air Boss (person in charge of all flight related activity at an air show) and the team. This allows the Team Lead to concentrate only on his flying. The coordinators do the show narration and manage the music score in accordance with the choreographed formations. Once the show is complete they get landing and taxi clearance for the team, pack up the radio equipment and join the rest of the team for autographs.

Public Affairs Officer

The team's public affairs officer is in charge of promoting the 431 (Air Demonstration) Squadron, educating the public about the Snowbirds, and coordinating all media and public relations activities for the team, including visits to schools, hospitals, social functions, and charity events. In addition to providing the team with media-awareness training, the public affairs officer also prepares all Snowbirds' print materials, such as brochures, posters, displays, and trading cards, updates the website, coordinates special projects, and looks after requests for the use of Snowbirds' images for commercial purposes.

Squadron Standards and Training Officer

As the title suggests, the squadron standards and training officer is responsible for ensuring that the members of the 431 (Air Demonstration) Squadron maintain the required levels of pilot proficiency, competency, and standards. Further tasks include conducting annual pilot-proficiency checks, maintaining pilot-training files, training incoming squadron commanders and coordinators, preparing pilot candidates for tryouts, conducting test flights and functional checks as required by maintenance, and scheduling flights with maintenance.

Crew Chief

The crew chief is the senior aircraft maintenance supervisor and is key to the maintenance and repair of the show team's aircraft, providing the finest technicians in the forces with what they need to keep the team flying while it is on the road. The chief is the direct connection between the operations officer and the executive officer. He also liaises with the coordinators at every show site to ensure that maintenance requirements are met and that all safety measures are in place for the aircraft. Throughout the show season, the crew chief travels with the team in the #1 jet, piloted by the team lead.

Deputy Crew Chief

The deputy crew chief is second-in-command to the crew chief and assists in all maintenance matters while the team is on the road. When the chief is unavailable, the deputy chief makes the decisions. All maintenance is coordinated between the chief, the deputy chief, and the operations officer. The deputy chief is also responsible for maintaining discipline and the code of conduct (dress and deportment). The deputy is the go-between for the crew and the chief.

Lead Aviation Technician

The lead aviation technician is the "go to" team member for issues related to the aircraft: flight controls, fuel systems, smoke systems, engine, structures, and egress. The lead aviation tech decides on manpower requirements, hours, and impact on the operation of aviation-related repairs, in addition to looking after repairs, parts, and tools.

The lead aviation tech is also a VIC lead. (VIC is a three-plane, "V"-shaped formation, often seen when taking off and landing. "Triple VIC" refers to three rows of three aircraft, each row in a "V" formation.) This means that, while the team transits across country, he is responsible for recording all of the fuel amounts used by the #5, #8, and #9 planes on the daily aircraft logs. As well as maintaining these fuel records, he ensures that all maintenance paperwork for these planes is completed and that all unserviceable parts are returned through the proper supply chains. Once a week, he must send all the fuel receipts, any maintenance paperwork, and the daily flying logs to Moose Jaw for input into the database.

All aviation-related snags are reported to the lead aviation tech and then to the crew chief, who determines and assigns the proper corrective action.

Lead Avionics Technician

The lead avionics technician is the "go to" team member for issues related to avionics: instrumentation, communications, and navigation. The lead avionics tech decides on manpower requirements, hours, and impact on the operation of avionics-related repairs. He is also a VIC lead and is responsible for recording the fuel use for his VIC formation (the #4, #6, and #7 planes). All avionics-related snags are reported to the lead avionics tech and then to the crew chief, who determines and assigns the proper corrective action.

One or both of the lead techs are also responsible for shooting video of all the show practices and performances, as well as the pre-season practices at Comox and Moose Jaw. These videos have two purposes. The first is pilot debriefing. Immediately after each practice and performance, the pilots review the video and evaluate their flights. Second, in the event of an incident, the video is quarantined and becomes part of the investigation.

Both the lead aviation and the lead avionics positions are held for one year. They are the result of an application process that includes intensive interviews. All technicians, including the crew chief and the deputy crew chief, are responsible not only for the serviceability and safety of each aircraft, but also for their particular plane's appearance.

The Home Team

While the show team is on the road, a talented "home team" of some fifty members provides indispensable support back in the two main hangars at 15 Wing Moose Jaw. Comprising a technical servicing and maintenance crew, a logistics crew, an administrative and financial services crew, a chaplain, and a flight surgeon, the home team does everything from launching and recovering jets, maintaining jets, and conducting periodic aircraft inspections, to manufacturing and repairing parts, carrying out non-destructive testing (e.g., x-ray), and developing and implementing pilot-training programs.

The home team is under the leadership of the deputy commanding officer while the show team is on the road, although the ultimate authority for all decisions rests with the commanding officer (the boss). Of course, while the team is at home, the deputy commanding officer is second-in-command, assisting the commanding officer at all times. The operations support officer and the squadron aircraft maintenance engineering officer report directly to the deputy commanding officer. The squadron standards and training officer reports to the commanding officer and to the deputy commanding officer.

Operations Support Officer

The operations support officer is responsible for providing logistical support to the squadron, including supply, traffic, resource management, and administrative services, both within the squadron and during the annual deployment. Among this officer's many tasks are: the timely and appropriate procurement, demand, receipt, storage, return, and distribution of material; ensuring the efficient and appropriate use of squadron financial resources; drafting the annual business plan; coordinating contracts for required services; ensuring the administrative requirements of the squadron are met in a timely and effective manner; and providing leadership and guidance to the operations support centre.

The operations support centre is made up of the operations support officer, the two team coordinators, the public affairs officer, and Marg Fowler (the operations support administrator). From an organizational perspective, it's not a linear chain of command, but more of a permanent working group of key team support staff. The goal of the group is to identify, plan, and execute all support elements of the team's annual deployment.

Squadron Standards and Training Officer

As the title suggests, the squadron standards and training officer is responsible for ensuring that the members of the 431 (Air Demonstration) Squadron maintain the required levels of pilot proficiency, competency, and standards. Further tasks include conducting annual pilot-proficiency checks, maintaining pilot-training files, training incoming squadron commanders and coordinators, preparing pilot candidates for tryouts, conducting test flights and functional checks as required by maintenance, and scheduling flights with maintenance.

Squadron Aircraft Maintenance Engineering Officer

The squadron aircraft maintenance engineering officer is responsible for the effective planning, organization, and conduct of all aircraft-maintenance functions. This includes developing and implementing all aircraft-maintenance policies for the squadron; ensuring the security of aircraft and equipment at all times; performing quality control of work carried out; ensuring adequate parts are available and maintained at home and off base; and ensuring inventory items are maintained and up-to-date.

The Maintenance Crew

Maintenance is divided into two major components: aircraft-maintenance production and aircraft-maintenance support.

Three teams are responsible for maintenance production:

- **Servicing:** Led by the crew chief, this team is mainly responsible for launching and recovering the jets.
- **Periodics:** This team conducts periodic aircraft inspections (every 400 hours of flying), during which the jets are stripped, inspected, and put back together.
- **Workshop:** This team of aircraft structures' technicians manufactures and/or repairs parts and does paint touch-ups on the jets.

The maintenance-support team is responsible for numerous areas, including non-destructive testing, tool control, the component shop, the engine bay, safety systems, the battery shop, log control, maintenance research, and the avionics labs. The team also includes a telecommunications information specialist.

The Canadian Forces Snowbirds are the only military-jet aerobatic team in the world that does not rely on support aircraft. The aviation technicians are responsible for flight controls, fuel systems, smoke systems, engine, structures, and egress. The avionics technicians are responsible for instrumentation, communications, and navigation.

The Aircraft and Flight Formations

The Canadair CT-114 Tutor

The Snowbirds fly the Canadair CT-114 Tutor, a Canadian-built jet that was used by the Canadian Forces as its basic pilot-training aircraft until 2000. With its high manoeuvrability and relatively slow speed, the Tutor is ideally suited to the formations and aerobatics performed by the Snowbirds.

Originally designated the CL41-A, the Tutor weighs approximately 3,260 kilograms (7,170 pounds). It is powered by a General Electric J-85 Axial Flow Turbo jet engine that produces 2,700 pounds of thrust. Top speed of the aircraft, with smoke tanks attached, is 412 knots (755 km/h or 470 mph). The plane has a fuel capacity of 1,173 litres (310 US gallons) and a cruising range of about 563 kilometres (350 miles). The Tutor has a turn rate approximately three times that of a CF-18.

The basic Tutor is only slightly modified for use by the Snowbirds. Modifications include a smoke-generating system, a unique paint scheme for added crowd appeal, and a highly tuned engine to enhance engine response in low-level flying. There are currently twenty CT-114 Tutors in the Snowbirds' active inventory.

The Tutor will remain the Snowbirds' aircraft for the immediate future. However, as the Tutors age, alternative aircraft are being considered.

Flight Formations

Formation flying is what the Snowbirds are all about. Performing amazing aerobatics while maintaining a "tight" formation is what people are there to see. So how does a Snowbirds performance come to be? The team commander (the Boss) is responsible for the show content. Each year the show changes slightly to make sure the audience always sees something new. When there is a change of command, the show usually goes through a more radical change to exhibit the personality of the new commander.

The show team is made up of nine aircraft. There are seven main formation aircraft and two solo aircraft. The show is basically a series of manoeuvres either by Snowbirds #1 through #7, by the solos (#8 and #9), or by all nine aircraft.

Depending on the weather conditions, the Snowbirds fly a High Show, a Low Show, or a Flat Show. The High Show is the full performance, as originally intended, with all manoeuvres included. To fly a High Show, the minimum cloud ceiling requirement is 1,350 metres (4,500 feet) and visibility must be 8 kilometres (5 miles). To fly a Low Show, the cloud ceiling must be at least 450 metres (1,500 feet) and visibility must be 8 kilometres (5 miles). A Flat Show needs a minimum ceiling of 300 metres (1,000 feet) and visibility of 5 kilometres (3 miles). No show is flown if the ceiling is below 300 metres or if visibility is less than 5 kilometres.

Currently, there are approximately forty formations in the Snowbirds' inventory. Their inventory is a combination of standard aerobatic formations, modified standard formations, and original creations. Once the formations are set, it becomes a question of how to incorporate them into the show.

Seven or nine planes? Loop or roll? Topside pass (where the tops of the planes are exposed to the audience) or bottom-side pass (where the bottoms of the planes are exposed)? A manoeuvre can be a single formation or a combination of several. Recommendations for new show formations and manoeuvres can come from anyone in the squadron, pilots and non-pilots alike. For example, Sergeant Luc Labrecque, the chief clerk, suggested a modification to the Draken Split that was adopted by the team. Ideas also come from outside the squadron. As Lead Solo Chuck Mallett told me: "We certainly have been influenced by other teams (most notably the Red Arrows) in some of the formations we fly. At the same time, they have been influenced by us. Three years ago, we watched the Reds perform in Toronto and liked one particular manoeuvre so much (the Four-plane Lag-back Cross) that we decided to change our own version of it from three airplanes to four. We altered it the following year as well, adding a fifth plane."

Each Snowbird air display is divided into three distinct phases:
- The Opener – featuring nine-plane formations
- The Integrated Portion – featuring a mix of solos and formations of up to seven planes
- The Closer – once again featuring nine-plane formations

The distance between each Snowbird jet in many of the formations is about 1.2 metres (4 feet). When flying at a speed of 600 kilometres (375 miles) per hour, the pilots require a large amount of skill to maintain this distance throughout a performance. Some formations actually have a wing overlap of several feet! The solos aim to be approximately 10 metres (33 feet) apart when they cross. At 600 kilometres per hour, the closure speed of these jets is very close to the speed of sound.

The 2004 High Show featured the following manoeuvres (solo manoeuvres are noted in italics):

Inverted Wedge to Big Diamond Loop
Big Diamond Roll and Loop
Maple Split

Knife Edge Pass — Cuban Reverse
Co 360 — Inverted Push

Card 7 Topside
Double Diamond Roll

Feather Loop (with *Solo cross*)
Feather 360 (*Solos rejoin*)

Concorde Loop
Concorde Burst

Split "S" Reverse — Inverted/Upright Cross
Vertical Reverse — Co Loop — Pigtail Exit

Downward Burst

Tuckaway Cross — Pretzel Reverse
Level Roll — Cobra Roll

Line Abreast Roll and Loop

4-Way Cross

Heart

Lag-back Cross

Mirror Roll

Echelon in Review (planes #7, #6, and #5)

Double Take

Double Inverted

Vic to Wedge to Arrow Loop
Arrow Wrap to Double Diamond to Swept 7

Solos rejoin to Big Arrow Loop

Vulcan to Big Diamond Loop

Big Diamond Wrap

Nine-plane Line Abreast over crowd

Although everyone has input into the music that is used for a show, Chuck Mallett put it all together during the three years he flew as a Snowbird. Here are a few comments from Chuck about how the music is chosen.

It is completely up to the team members what music gets used. We try to use music that supports the mood we feel is most appropriate to the different elements of the show—graceful music for large formations and more-driving rock music for the solos and the integrated portion of the show.

We also try to use as much Canadian content as possible. Finally, we try to pick music that "goes together" to keep the show from being too much of a mishmash of musical styles.

While not all teams have spent as much time on this as I did, I worked hard to make the music in sync with the show all three years I was on the team. I made a list of cues for the co-coordinators to start the tracks at specific times. I even spent time editing songs to make them fit with various manoeuvres. It is very satisfying when "Conviction of the Heart," by Kenny Loggins, hits its chorus right at the moment the formation splits apart for the Maple Split. It takes a great deal of time to design the music to do that. Of course, we can't hear the music as we fly, but we always get to hear it when we watch the tape after each show.

We try to pick music that we like (we have to hear it every time we debrief) and that we think our target audience will like. The Snowbirds are a recruiting tool, so the key demographic is the late teens and early twenties. This year the most popular song in the show is "You and I (were meant to fly)," by Celine Dion. It was written for an Air Canada ad campaign, but we've made it our own.

David Foster and Steven Vitali have both written music for the team with their songs "Flight of the Snowbirds" and "In Flight," respectively. Only the latter was used in the 2005 show. Also, following the accident on 10 December 2004, a friend of Snowbird #7, named Eliot Pister, wrote a song for the team called "Open Skies for Miles." We used that song in the 2005 show.

The Snowbirds' show is designed to have something happening in front of the crowd at all times. Their presentation of skilled aerobatics, narration, and music continues to thrill audiences across Canada and the United States.

Diagrams of some of the more popular formations flown by the Snowbirds are found below.

Who's Who in the Air?

Snowbird #1 — Team Lead

Snowbird #2 — Inner Right Wing

Snowbird #3 — Inner Left Wing

Snowbird #4 — First Line Astern

Snowbird #5 — Second Line Astern

Snowbird #6 — Outer Right Wing

Snowbird #7 — Outer Left Wing

Snowbird #8 — Opposing Solo

Snowbird #9 — Lead Solo

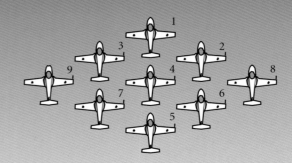

Big Diamond

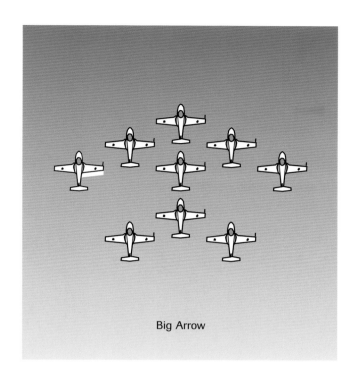

Big Arrow

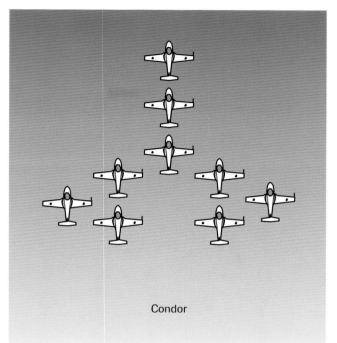

Condor

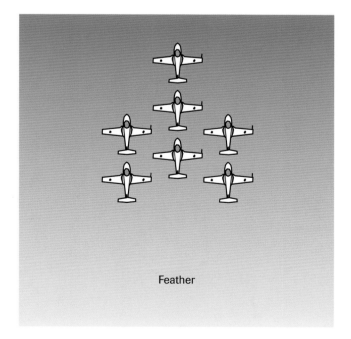

Feather

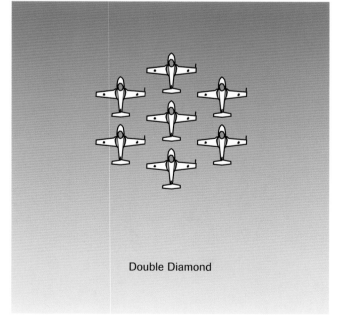

Double Diamond

43

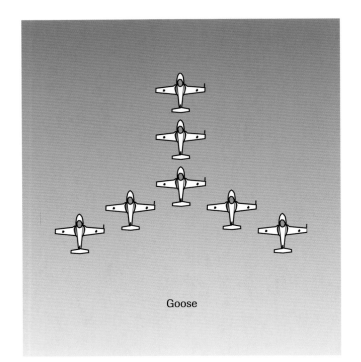

Goose

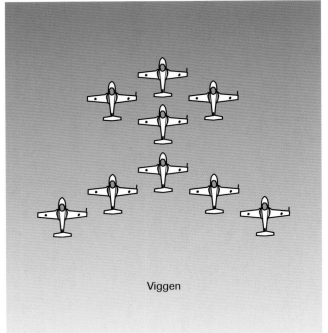

Viggen

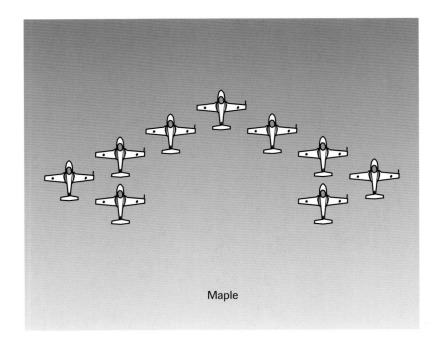

Maple

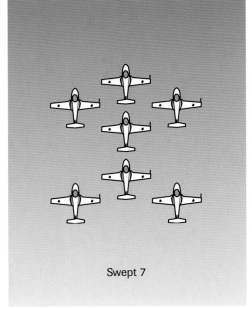

Swept 7

44

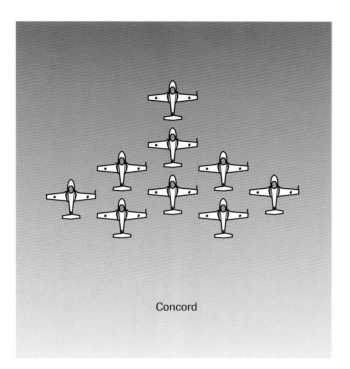

Concord

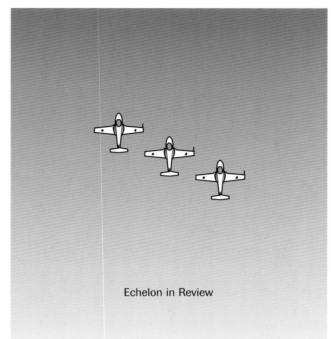

Echelon in Review

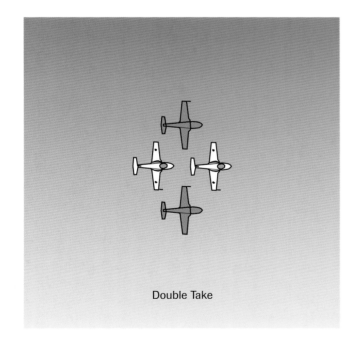

Double Take

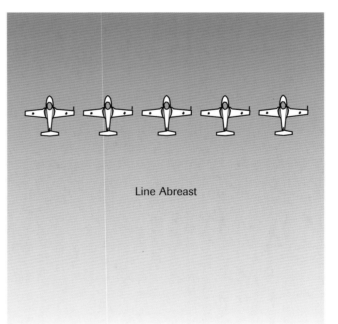

Line Abreast

45

On the Road

Before the Show

The first to leave Moose Jaw are members of the ground crew, who depart in the support van with enough lead time to arrive at the show site at about the same time as the airplanes do. Next, Snowbirds #10 and #11, the team coordinators, take off. They will arrive two to three hours before the main formation. They measure and mark aircraft parking positions for the jets, prepare to brief the pilots as soon as they land and exit their planes, and ensure that the show site has met all of its contractual obligations. For weekend shows, the arrival date is usually Thursday. For mid-week shows, it is usually Tuesday.

After arriving at a new show site and taxiing to their assigned parking positions, the Snowbird pilots leave their cockpits, shake hands, and proceed to the #5 plane, where the "over wing" briefing takes place. Pilots and technicians are briefed together about airport/air-base layout, accommodations, rental cars, media appearances, and the like. After the general briefing, the technicians move to the other wing to discuss technical issues, while the pilots, the coordinators, and the public affairs officer stay where they are to discuss flying issues.

Once the team members settle in, they get ready for a Thursday practice. They also plan any hospital or school visits. Friday is either a practice day or a performance day, which usually ends with a social function to attend in the evening. Alcohol restrictions are put into place.

On the Day of the Show

On show day, the first order of business is the Air Show brief organized by the air show staff. Each show site will have a Snowbirds' show pilot assigned to it. The show pilot's duties include attending this brief and bringing relevant information back to the Snowbirds' team briefing. The pilots, coordinators, and public affairs officer attend the team briefing.

The team briefing includes:
- weather briefing and NOTAMS ("notices to airmen" containing information about the establishment of, condition of, or change in any aeronautical facility, service, procedure, or hazard on the site)
- aircraft lineup
- standard fuel for mission (Pilots will call a "Joker" when fuel reaches 1,000 pounds and "Bingo" when it reaches 600 pounds.)
- start, taxi, and takeoff procedures
- recovery and landing procedures
- turn-in (simultaneous or individual) and shutdown procedures
- abort procedures and the emergency-of-the-day

(During each briefing session, an emergency scenario is presented and each pilot must give an appropriate response—do they continue with the takeoff, or the manoeuvre, or do they safely abort?)
- mission profile (The entire mission's radio transmissions are called by the Boss, which allows each pilot to visualize the performance before flying it.)
- additional business such as media flights, media ride-alongs, or formation flying with other military aircraft such as the Canadian Demo CF-18.

In the meantime, the ground crew preps the aircraft for the upcoming performance, unpacking— opening the aircraft canopy, removing intake covers, etc.—inspecting, and cleaning each one. The crew also decides whether or not they need to press the spare planes into service. Another key part of the pre-flight show preparation is the "FOD" (Foreign Object Damage) walk, during which ground technicians walk down the ramp area looking for foreign objects that could cause damage if jets roll over them or if they are sucked into the jet intakes.

The Show

When it's time for the show, if the planes are parked out of the audience's sight, the pilots simply proceed to their aircraft, perform visual inspections to ensure all is in order, enter their jets, and conduct a pre-flight check. If the crowd can see the parked planes, the pilots and ground crew formally proceed to their aircraft, technicians dressed in blue and pilots in red. First, the technicians march smartly to their respective planes, while the pilots stand at ease. Then, the pilots march in three lines of three, with each pilot breaking off to face the plane's technician. They exchange salutes and shake hands before completing a final inspection and entering the cockpit.

As the planes fire up, each technician proceeds to a point directly in front of his or her plane to perform a four-finger check. First check, conducted standing, is of the speed brakes (hydraulic flaps on each side of the plane that, when activated, serve as brakes in the air). Second check, conducted kneeling, is of the flaps. Third check, again conducted standing, is of the pin flag that indicates the ejection seat is armed. Fourth check, also conducted standing, is of the lights. Then, providing there are no problems, the technician gives the thumbs up and the jet is ready to roll.

Meanwhile, the coordinators confirm that restricted airspace is active and get takeoff and taxi clearance for the team. They are the only point of contact between the air boss (the person in charge of all air-show performance activity) and the team. This allows the team lead to concentrate on flying.

Now the planes either turn out one by one to follow the team lead or all turn out simultaneously. The crew chief and deputy crew chief position themselves down the ramp and perform a final visual inspection, known as the "last chance" check. Then, it's thumbs up and go!

After takeoff, the pilots fly in a Triple Vic formation (3 by 3) to a remote area of the sky, out of sight of the audience. Once there, the team lead breaks off and does a visual inspection of all the planes. He then calls for the "shake out." Each plane performs a roll to inverted, followed by a 5g climb (pilots experience five times the normal pull of gravity) and a -2g "push" (dive). Finally, a smoke check is performed. If everything checks out okay, it's show time.

On the ground, the coordinators warm up the crowd by presenting background information on the history of the Snowbirds, team statistics, details of show manoeuvres, and dedications to the audience. The next voice you hear is the commander as he addresses the crowd from the cockpit of Snowbird #1. He introduces himself, greets the crowd, announces the show dedication, and explains any changes that may have been made to the show.

Without warning, the Snowbirds zoom over the crowd in the show's opening formation and there is no turning back. The crowd cheers and, for the next thirty minutes, all eyes are fixed on the red, white, and blue planes flying overhead. Snowbirds #1 through #7 fly in formation, performing spectacular loops and rolls, while the two solo pilots execute a series of unbelievable passes. At times, the separation between planes seems impossibly close. On the ground, the coordinators manage the music score in accordance with the choreographed formations. On each approach, the planes turn on the white smoke, which helps define the entire manoeuvre to the audience. It's almost as if the Snowbirds are painting the sky. They pass right before the crowd, then climb almost out of sight. The Snowbirds plan each performance so there is never a dull moment. As soon as one pass or loop is completed, another move is being performed. There is always something happening in front of the audience so that performances appear seamless and smooth from start to finish. From lyrical, dance-like formations to heart-pounding, high-speed solo passes, the team puts on an incredible show.

After the Show

After a performance that always leaves the crowd cheering, the ground crew gathers with the pilots for an over-wing briefing at the wing of the #5 jet. They go through the serviceability of each jet with the pilots; the pilots then sign off on the aircraft servicing set, which records hours flown and serviceability. The ground crew remains to discuss any technical aircraft problems and what resources will be required to bring jets back on line. The crew chief sets the priorities if repairs are required and ensures that the ground crew works through continuously until all the aircraft are serviceable again.

After their over-wing briefing with the ground crew, the pilots meet with their dedicated fans, young and old alike. The fans come out for autographs and a chance to meet their heroes. Of course, the team is always happy to oblige. At one point or another during this project, each and every pilot told me that this is definitely one of the "perks" of being with the Snowbirds. The same goes for the technicians. They truly enjoy the opportunity to meet their fans. I was surprised at the extent of their fan base.

In Canada, it's just as you would expect—they are truly a Canadian icon, and Canadians from coast to coast are proud to call them their own. But the response to the team in the United States is equally impressive. Fans line up at every air show for a chance to meet Canada's Snowbirds. There is no end to web-sites from around the world that feature the Snowbirds, and a visit to the Snowbirds' official website: (http://www.snowbirds.dnd.ca) shows fan mail from every corner of the globe.

Show sites are not the only place the Snowbirds meet their fans. The pilots and technicians also make innumerable public appearances at hospitals, schools, and many charity events where fans invariably have interesting stories to tell. During one particular hospital visit, the Snowbirds met a small boy with a broken arm. When asked how he had broken it, the boy said he had fallen off the porch while watching the Snowbirds fly over the family home!

From the time the team touches down at a new location until they leave the autograph line after the last performance, there is little time to relax, so Mondays are designated as days off. Team members can recuperate from a show however they choose. Some stay at the hotel and relax. Others play a round of golf or do some sightseeing. Some even squeeze in one more public appearance on their day off. Whatever they choose to do, the next day the team is in the air once again, on their way to the next show site.

The Photographs

The Canadian-built CT-114 Tutor sits on the tarmac at Abbotsford, British Columbia, with Mount Baker in the background.

The *Big Arrow* over
the harbour at Comox,
British Columbia.

It's early and it's cold as another
Snowbird jet heads to the flight line
during new-pilot tryouts.

Left: *Nine-Plane Abreast!*

Card 7

Dramatic *Lag-back Cross*

Captain Miles Selby discusses a manoeuvre with Snowbird candidate Captain Mike French. Snowbird #3, Captain Cory Blakely, observes.

The *Condor*

Snowbird pilot candidates head to their planes for a final day of flight testing.

Planes roll for the final tryout flight. Later in the day, the list of successful candidates is announced at a ceremony held in the Snowbirds Lounge.

Planes appear slightly out of position during the *Maple Split* manoeuvre early in the training session at 19 Wing Comox. Within two weeks, the formations will be "tight" and ready for the Acceptance Show.

Solos on the rejoin, with the Comox Glacier in the background.

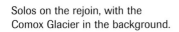

The *Nine-Plane Line Abreast* formation flies over
the ground crew during the Acceptance Show.

The *Goose* takes
to the skies.

Major General Marc J. Dumais
and Colonel Alain Boyer watch the
Acceptance Show at 15 Wing Moose
Jaw. The general must approve the
show and team itinerary before
signing documents that give the
Snowbirds permission to commence
the show season.

Opposite page: *Four-Way Cross*

Opposite page: Prior to departing for each segment of the show itinerary, called a "swing," the team stands around the Snowbirds' crest, painted on a hangar floor, and takes part in a group prayer.

Below: Master Corporal Mike Underwood's expertise is obvious as he packs a parachute.

Left: Corporal Robert Kilbride hangs parachutes for a periodic "airing out." Parachutes undergo inspection and are then repacked and certified "ready for use."

Captain Patrick Gobeil, Snowbird #6, prepares for an air show while at home between "swings."

Captain Gobeil focuses on details while preparing for the Saskatoon Air Show.

Upward Burst

Helmets and chute packs are "ready to go."

An early morning rollout for yet another practice is a familiar start to the day for the Snowbirds.

Left: A quiet moment. Show planes 1–9, coordinators 10 and 11, and the standards number 12, photographed at dawn.

Above: Sometimes you just have to stop what you are doing and watch the "other guys."

Dramatic clouds provide a backdrop for a dynamic portrait of the CT-114 Tutor.

Snowbird #1 leads the team in as they arrive at a new show location.

After marking the pavement for each jet prior to the team's arrival at an airport, the team coordinators guide the jets to their parking positions. Here, Captain Lyle Holbrook shepherds a plane to its position.

Below: During "over wing" briefings, Snowbird team members go over the "show sheets," which describe important show and non-show information, such as schedules and accommodations.

Above: Site Coordinator Captain Gavin Crouch discusses logistics at the "over wing" briefing, held immediately after the team's arrival.

Above: Pilots and ground crew go over the show sheets for their visit to Andrews Air Force Base.

Left: Sometimes the worst weather makes for the best skies. Here, the team works its magic in front of a major storm system that continues to build.

Above: After the initial "over wing" briefing, which includes both pilots and technicians, the two groups split into separate briefings, one over each wing, to discuss issues specific to their own group.

After arriving at a new airfield, the Tutors are refuelled. Note the pilot's luggage on the wing.

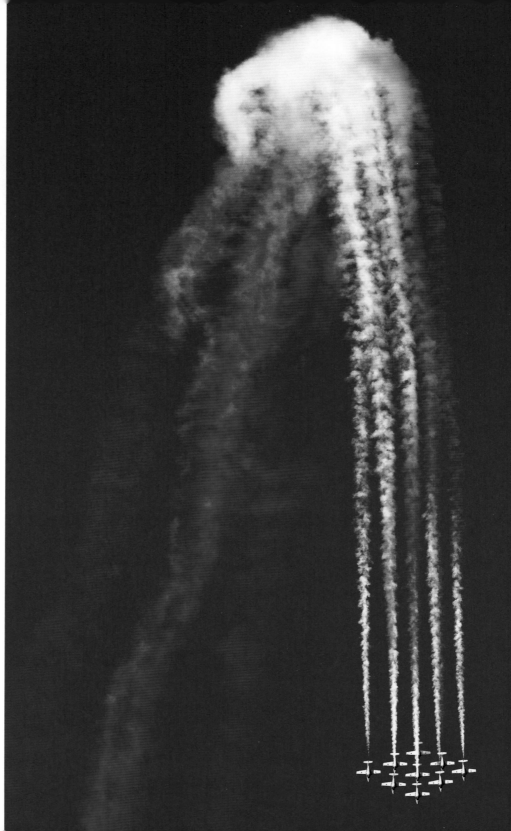

Big Diamond, up and down

Far left: Snowbird jets stand ready on the tarmac at 19 Wing Comox.

Left: Technicians work to replace the smoke lines on Snowbird #8.

Below: *Feather*, above the storm clouds

Right: Lead Avionics Technician Corporal Dave Talbot makes observations at the "Identify Friend or Foe" (IFF) test bench.

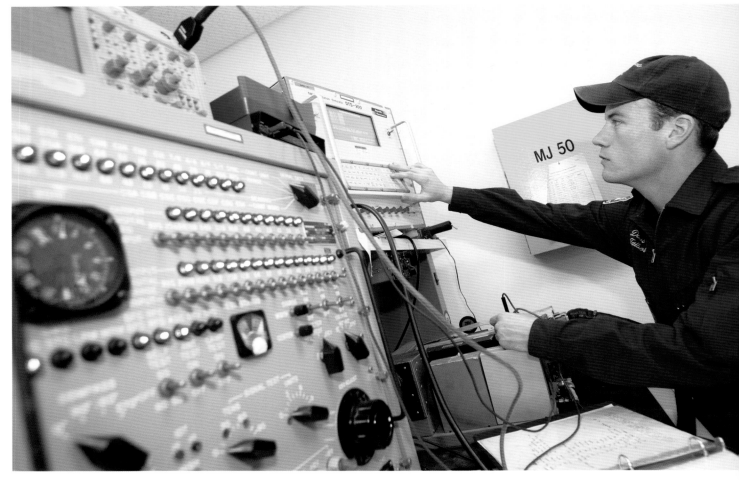

Below: Corporal Claude Aucoin reworks the rivets during routine maintenance on one of the Snowbird jets.

Corporal Brian Phillips and Corporal Mirko Robertson prepare an engine for testing.

Opposite page: The "business end" of a CT-114 Tutor.

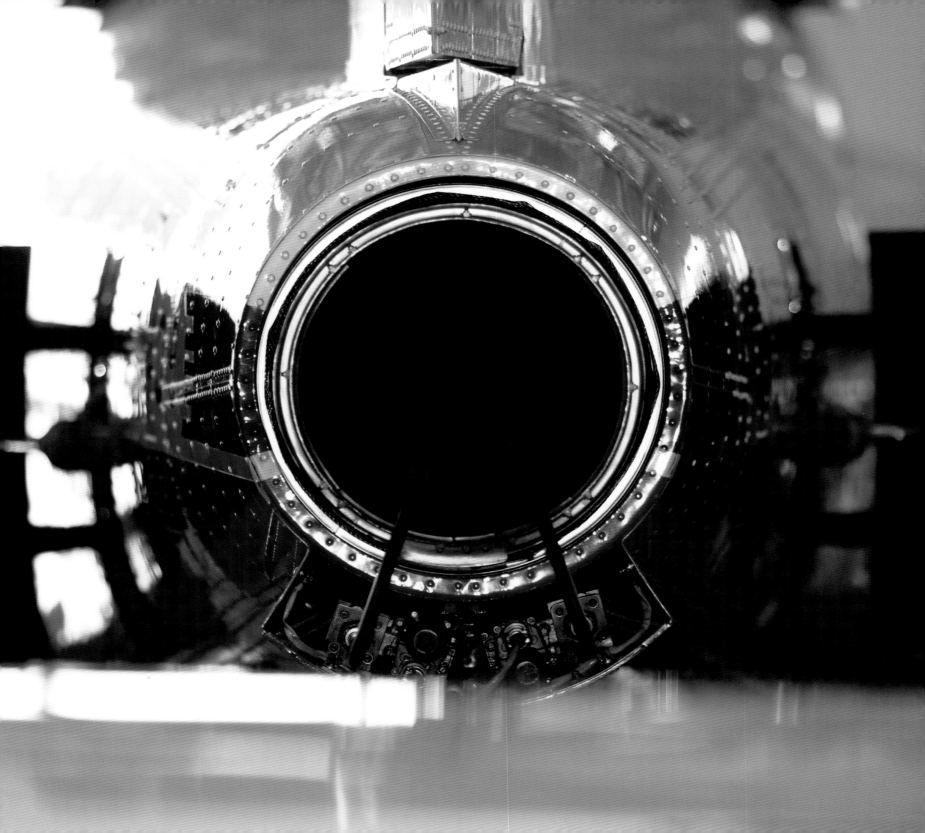

Above: Nine-Plane Line Abreast

Right: A view inside the Tutor's cockpit. Because the Tutor was originally used as a flight trainer, identical controls can be found on the left and right sides of the cockpit. A toggle switch next to the UHF indicator determines which controls are active.

Far right: The deputy crew chief and lead aviation technician make some adjustments inside a jet's battery compartment, with Mount Baker in the background.

Snowbird pilots discuss the issues of the day at a pre-show briefing. The end-of-performance debriefing takes place at the same location. Note the members of the USAF Thunderbirds in the background.

Deputy Crew Chief Master Corporal Darrell Fournier (r) and Lead Aviation Technician Corporal Ryan Willett (l) discuss the day's maintenance requirements.

Draken Split

Big Arrow

Left: Corporal Richard Pilon wipes down the smoke nozzle area on Snowbird #9.

Above: Snowbirds #8 and #9 perform the *Double Inverted Pass*.

Big Diamond, over the Strait of Georgia, British Columbia.

While fuel trucks wait, the show technicians position the aircraft into a perfect line in preparation for an air show.

Inverted Big Diamond

Crew Chief Sergeant Dave Scharf wipes down Snowbird #1. The U.S. Navy Blue Angels' flight line can be seen in the background.

Above: The technicians perform a "FOD" (Foreign Object Damage) walk, looking for any foreign objects that may be sucked into a jet intake or blown into another aircraft when the Tutors taxi for takeoff and return.

Middle: The show technicians march to the planes just prior to an air show.

Right: The show pilots are ready to march in formation to their planes.

Five-Plane Line Abreast

Snowbird Captain Andy Mackay breaks off from the show pilots' formation to board his own aircraft.

As pilots meet their technicians, a salute and a handshake are in order before they proceed to their aircraft.

When the air show audience has no direct view of the flight line, the show team forgoes the formal march out to their jets.

Echelon in Review

Opposite page: Captain Patrick Gobeil inspects his plane prior to the day's performance. Corporal Mirko Robertson looks on.

D/Crew Chief ✈ MCpl Darrell Fournier

The Snowbirds roll for another spectacular performance.

The team waits at the end of the runway.

Let the show begin with a *Triple Vic* takeoff.

Right: *Big Diamond* without Snowbird #4.

Opposite page, top right: Under the watchful eye of Master Corporal Shawn Stone, the Snowbirds taxi to the runway in preparation for a performance.

Opposite page, top left: Crew Chief Sergeant Dave Scharf gives a "thumbs up" during the "last chance check."

Opposite page: Snowbird pilots go through the "4-Finger" check just prior to a performance at the Abbotsford Air Show.

Technicians conduct a quick review of the morning's activities after the planes have "rolled."

Above: Snowbird coordinators Gavin Crouch and Lyle Holbrook and Public Affairs Officer Captain Stephanie Walker watch with interest during a performance at 15 Wing Moose Jaw.

Below: A Snowbirds' fan captures the "Heart," a crowd favourite, at the 2003 Dayton Air Show, in Ohio, which celebrated one hundred years of powered flight.

Opposite page: Area students and parents watch the Snowbirds perform at 15 Wing Moose Jaw.

Back side of the *Loop*, as seen from the air.

The team heads back to the base after performing manoeuvres.

Snowbird #5, Major Chris Hope, checks
his position on a tight formation turn.

Snowbirds are inverted
during the *Big Diamond*.

A large crowd enjoys the Snowbird performance at the 2003 Dayton Air Show in Ohio.

Double Take

Air cadets watch a Snowbird
practice at the Red Deer Air
Show in Alberta.

An important task for one of the
lead technicians is to videotape
each performance. These tapes
are scrutinized by the show team
during the day's debriefing.

The *Big Diamond* passes behind
a group of Snowbird technicians.

The Snowbirds end one of
their shows with *Nine Planes
Line Abreast*.

The team taxis back to the
ramp after performing in front
of an appreciative audience.

Close pass shot from *Inside the Box*

Opposite page: *Big Diamond*, missing Snowbird #4, with Snowbird #5 pulled forward to fill the empty slot.

Opposite page:
Five-Plane Line Abreast

Big Diamond, missing Snowbird #2, during a sunset show at White Rock, British Columbia.

The Snowbirds are delighted to sign autographs at the Halifax Air Show.

Opposite page: After each performance, the team takes part in the long-standing tradition of shaking hands with each other to signify a job well done.

Another Snowbirds' handshake line at the end of a performance.

Majors Will and McLean, the outgoing and incoming bosses, respectively, embrace after the last show of the season.

The Snowbirds are delighted to sign autographs at the Halifax Air Show.

Opposite page: After each performance, the team takes part in the long-standing tradition of shaking hands with each other to signify a job well done.

Another Snowbirds' handshake line at the end of a performance.

Majors Will and McLean, the outgoing and incoming bosses, respectively, embrace after the last show of the season.

The Snowbirds and U.S. Navy Blue Angels share an autograph line at Andrews Air Force Base, the "Home of Air Force One," near Washington, DC.

Youngsters, especially,
covet Snowbirds' autographs.

Opposite page: *Concorde Roll*

Big Diamond,
climbing for the heavens.

The Snowbirds gather at jet
#5 for a post-performance
"over wing" debriefing.

Late in the afternoon, the
team debriefs a performance
at the Halifax Air Show.

Miss Teen Canada and the Snowbirds
team record a message for the Canadian
men and women serving overseas.

Major Steve Will, Snowbird #1, hams
it up for the camera during a relaxed
moment between performances.

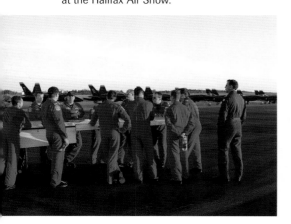

Technician ✈ Cpl Guy Palin

Four-Plane Stack

Opposite page: Invitations for ride-alongs are an excellent way to build relationships and generate goodwill, both in the community and with aerobatics team members from around the world. Snowbird #7, Captain Steve Chadwick, is ready to take USAF Thunderbird #4, Major Matt Beckley, for a ride.

A "gaggle" shot of ride-along participants at the Cold Lake Air Show, Alberta.

Corporal Cameron Simms tests a Tactical Air Navigation (TACAN) device, an ultra-high-frequency electronic navigation aid that provides suitably equipped aircraft with a continuous indication of bearing and distance to the TACAN station.

A Tutor undergoing scheduled maintenance is a view of the jet never seen by the air show audience.

Sergeant Grant Beeber and Corporal Laurie Walsh are two of the supply techs who help ensure necessary parts are on hand both at home and on the road.

A key part of each show swing is the "goodie bag" that each pilot receives. It contains a "swing card," a small laminated card with show dates and vital information for each air show during that particular swing, and giveaways such as pins, cards, and stickers. Here, Operations Support Assistant Marg Fowler and Corporal Jenn Lyons assemble goodie bags.

Opposite page: Captain Chuck Mallett rolls his #9 jet, initiating the *Five-Plane Lag-back Cross*.

Double Diamond, along Air Force Beach, Comox, British Columbia.

Maple Split break, before the storm.

Vic Pass

Precision flying at its best!

Hospital visits across Canada are a regular part of the Snowbirds' schedule.

Opposite page: Fans get "up close and personal" during one of the many Snowbirds social functions during the season.

Being a Snowbird fan has no age limitation. Ninety-four-year-old Alex Bruce watches the Snowbirds fly past each year at the Captain Michael VandenBos Public School near Toronto, Ontario.

The Snowbirds perform a fly-past at the Captain Michael VandenBos Public School near Toronto, Ontario. The school was named for the Snowbird who lost his life during a practice in 1998.

Big Diamond, in the skies over Abbotsford, British Columbia.

Opposite page: Master Corporal Darrell Fournier shows
Pierce Brooks the "driver's seat" during the team's visit to
the Child Foundation in Vancouver, British Columbia.

Snowbirds solos #8 and #9 fly the
Mirror Roll, canopy to canopy.

Opposite page: Solos thrill the crowd
with an exciting *Knife-edge Pass*.

Opposite page: *Maple Split*

Master Corporal Terry Allain does his daily entries in the plane's logbook. A U.S. Navy Blue Angels F/A-18 Hornet is in the background.

Warrant Officer Jim Flach documents a bird strike.

The air show crowd long gone, Corporal Ryan Willett and Corporal Dave Talbot replace a fuel-boost pump, in the light of a setting sun.

Corporal Jean-Pierre Bérubé fills the smoke tanks with diesel fuel, at sunset in Halifax, Nova Scotia.

Opposite page: The *Big Diamond* formation flies along the Blue Angels flight line. A large thunderstorm that almost cancelled the Snowbirds performance moves out of the area.

Feather, with solos rejoining, above Cold Lake, Alberta.

Solo Snowbird #8 on the re-form, with forest-fire smoke in the background.

Opposite page: *Arrow*

Left: Snowbirds fly the *Big Vic*
formation over the pier at
White Rock, British Columbia.

Right: The end of day at Hangar 7,
home of the Canadian Forces Snowbirds,
15 Wing Moose Jaw, Saskatchewan.

Sometimes the technicians miss scheduled
evening social events because they
"don't leave until the job is done."

Big Arrow

Afterword

On 15 October 2004, there was a Change of Command ceremony at 15 Wing Moose Jaw. It signalled both a change and a continuation. That day, Major Steve Will relinquished command of the squadron to Major Ian McLean. Major McLean, who would lead the 431 (Air Demonstration) Squadron for the next three years, reflected on what it means to be part of the Snowbirds' team.

It is a great honour and a privilege to take command of a squadron with the rich history of 431 Air Demonstration Squadron. The 35th anniversary season forces each serving member to examine that history and discover his or her place within this rich tapestry. I have found that becoming the commanding officer and team lead requires this same introspection and path of discovery within this "Tradition of Excellence." Initially, assuming command is a daunting task. My predecessor, Major Steve Will, is a very talented leader and an excellent pilot. His departure, as I'm sure has occurred each time in the past, left a huge void and a very big pair of shoes to fill. The challenge is surmountable only because new leads are guided by the existing team of consummate professionals that form the Snowbirds.

Unfortunately, just prior to Christmas 2004, we collectively suffered further challenges when we experienced the tragic loss of Captain Miles Selby, our new Opposing Solo. As our focal point following the accident, I chose our Air Force motto *Per Ardua Ad Astra*, "Through Adversity to the Stars." In using this theme, the 2005 Snowbirds have faced adversity of the worst order, climbed back into the red and white jets that continue as a national icon, and formed another show deserving of the Snowbird name. The Snowbirds continue to transcend challenges and by doing so allow all Canadians to share in the Snowbird experience. I believe that in our perseverance we have demonstrated the dedication, pride, and professionalism inherent in all Canadian Forces members. In overcoming the myriad challenges of our past training season, the 2005 Snowbirds' team has earned its place within the Snowbirds' tapestry. To command such a unit is the reward of being Snowbird #1.

Major I. W. McLean
CO 431 (Air Demonstration) Squadron
The Hatiten Ronteriios—Warriors of the Air

Postscript *Show Pilot Biographies*

Major Steve Will ("Swill"), Snowbird #1
(Lieutenant Colonel Steve Will as of
December 2005)

Major Stephen Will *("Swill") Team Lead 2002 / 2003 / 2004, Snowbird #1*

Major Will is from North Bay, Ontario. After enrolling in the Canadian Forces in 1983 and receiving his wings in 1986, Major Will was posted to 15 Wing Moose Jaw, Saskatchewan, as a flying instructor. In 1988, he was selected to fly as Snowbird #3 in the Inner Left Wing position.

After a two-year tour with the Snowbirds, Major Will was selected for fighter-pilot training on the CF-5 Freedom Fighter and the CF-18 Hornet and, in 1991, was posted to 439 "Fangs of Death" Tactical Fighter Squadron in Germany to fly the CF-18 operationally.

In 1992, he was posted back to Canada to 441 Squadron in Cold Lake, Alberta. In 1996, Major Will served with 2 Canadian Mechanized Brigade Group in Bosnia as an air liaison officer. Upon his return to Canada, he was posted to Fighter Group Headquarters in North Bay, Ontario, where he worked in Joint Operations.

In 1997, Major Will returned to 4 Wing Cold Lake, Alberta, as the chief of Wing Standards and Evaluation and as Officer Commanding Air Force Tactical Training Centre. Two years later, he participated in Operation Allied Force in Bosnia, in which he flew over fifty missions in a CF-18. Major Will returned once again to Canada in 2000 as the deputy commanding officer of 441 Squadron, where he remained until being posted in 2001 to 1 Canadian Air Division Headquarters in Winnipeg, Manitoba. Major Will assumed command of 431 (Air Demonstration) Squadron, the Snowbirds, in October 2001.

In 2005, Major Will was promoted to lieutenant colonel.

Major Ian McLean ("Manic") Team Lead 2005, Snowbird #1

Major McLean is from London, Ontario. After enrolling in the Canadian Forces in 1980 and completing Basic Officer Training, he took flight training on the CT-134 Musketeer and the CT-114 Tutor aircraft. Following his graduation in 1982, Major McLean was selected to fly the CC-130 Hercules transport aircraft at 435 Squadron in Edmonton, Alberta, where he performed in strategic, tactical, and search and rescue missions. In 1987, Major McLean was selected for fighter-pilot training. Upon completion of the CF-5 Freedom Fighter and the CF-18 Hornet courses, he was posted to Bagotville, Quebec, where he completed the first of two tours with 425 Squadron as a front-line fighter pilot.

In 1990, Major McLean was posted to Wing Operations in Cold Lake, Alberta, as deputy Maple Flag officer. As well as coordinating Maple Flag, he participated as an operations officer in the Gulf War. In 1993, Major McLean was posted to 441 Tactical Fighter Squadron in Cold Lake, where he completed a three-and-a-half-year tour,

again as a front-line pilot. During this time, he upgraded to mass attack lead. Upon completion of this tour, he was assigned to instruct on the CF-18 and moved to 410 Tactical Fighter Training Squadron, still in Cold Lake. Shortly after joining 410 Squadron, Major McLean successfully completed a tryout with the Snowbirds. For the 1998 and 1999 show seasons, he flew the #7 aircraft on the Outer Left Wing. Major McLean was then chosen for an exchange position with the Royal Air Force in High Wycombe, United Kingdom, where he spent two years as the chief of Master Air Attack Planning for the Royal Air Force Joint Force Air Component Headquarters. In this role, he participated in operations in Sierra Leone, aboard the carrier HMS *Illustrious*, and in Saudi Arabia, during the Afghanistan campaign following the events of 11 September 2001. Upon his return to Canada in 2002, Major McLean commenced his third operational Hornet tour as the squadron weapons and tactics officer at 425 Tactical Fighter Squadron in Bagotville.

Major Ian McLean ("Manic"), Snowbird #1

Captain Paul Couillard ("Coolio") Inner Right Wing 2003/2004/2005, Snowbird #2

Captain Couillard is from Montreal, Quebec. He joined the Canadian Forces in 1990 under the Officer Cadet Training Plan. After receiving his wings, Captain Couillard was posted to 423 Maritime Helicopter Squadron in Shearwater, Nova Scotia, where he flew the CH-124 Sea King helicopter. In 1999, he was posted to

2 Canadian Forces Flying Training School in Moose Jaw, Saskatchewan, as a flying instructor on the CT-114 Tutor. Captain Couillard subsequently switched to the CT-156 Harvard II, the NATO Flying Training in Canada program's new training aircraft.

Captain Paul Couillard ("Coolio"), Snowbird #2

Captain Chris Bard *("Bardo") Inner Left Wing 2002/2003, Snowbird #3*

431 Squadron Deputy Commanding Officer Major Stu McIntosh (l) and Captain Chris Bard ("Bardo"), Snowbird #3 (r)

Captain Bard is from Guelph, Ontario. He joined the Canadian Forces in 1988 under the Regular Officer Training Plan and graduated from the University of Toronto in 1992. After receiving his wings, Captain Bard was posted to 407 Maritime Patrol Squadron in Comox, British Columbia, where he flew the CP-140 Aurora long-range patrol aircraft. In 1998, he was posted to 2 Canadian Forces Flying Training School in Moose Jaw, Saskatchewan, as a flying instructor on the CT-114 Tutor. Captain Bard was subsequently selected to help with the transition from the Tutor to the CT-156 Harvard II, the NATO Flying Training in Canada program's new training aircraft.

Major Cory Blakely *("Flash") Inner Left Wing 2004/2005, Snowbird #3*

Major Cory Blakely ("Flash"), Snowbird #3

Captain Blakely is from Edmonton, Alberta. He joined the Canadian Forces in 1990 under the Community College Entry Plan for Pilots (CCEPP) and graduated with a diploma in Aviation Science from Mount Royal College in Calgary, Alberta, in 1991. After receiving his wings in 1994, Captain Blakely was posted to 434 Squadron in Greenwood, Nova Scotia, as a combat-support pilot on the CT-133 Silver Star. In 2000, he was posted to 2 Canadian Forces Flying Training School in Moose Jaw, Saskatchewan, to instruct on the CT-156 Harvard II, where he accumulated over 450 instructional flying hours.

Major Stephen Melanson *("Pup") First Line Astern 2003, Snowbird #4*

Major Stephen Melanson ("Pup"), Snowbird #4, signing autographs

Major Melanson is from Moncton, New Brunswick. After joining the Canadian Forces in 1985, he began his flying career as a Sea King helicopter pilot in 1989 with 423 Squadron in Shearwater, Nova Scotia. In 1993, he was posted to 2 Canadian Forces Flying Training School in Moose Jaw, Saskatchewan, where he achieved an A2 Qualified Flying Instructor rating on the CT-114 Tutor. In 1997, Major Melanson was selected to participate in an exchange with the Royal Air Force Central Flying School in the United Kingdom as a flying instructor, where he flew the Tucano. In 2000, Major Melanson began flying both the Harvard II and Hawk 115 aircraft with the NATO Flying Training in Canada program and finished his tour as chief flying instructor.

Captain Miles Selby *("Milhouse") First Line Astern 2004, Snowbird #4*

Captain Miles Selby ("Milhouse"), Snowbird #4

Captain Selby was from Tsawwassen, British Columbia. He joined the Canadian Forces in 1991 under the Regular Officer Training Plan and graduated from Royal Roads Military College in 1995. After receiving his wings, Captain Selby was selected for fighter-pilot training and was subsequently posted to 416 Tactical Fighter Squadron in Cold Lake, Alberta, where he flew the CF-18 Hornet. In 1999, Captain Selby flew several operational missions in Kosovo and returned the following year to fly peacekeeping missions over the Balkans. In the summer of 2001, Captain Selby was posted to 441 Tactical Fighter Squadron in Cold Lake, Alberta, remaining on the CF-18 Hornet. He attended the Tactical Leadership Program flying course in Florennes, Belgium, and then completed his mass attack lead upgrade in 2002.

During the last practice before the 2004 Christmas break, Miles tragically lost his life while practising at the Snowbirds' home base. Miles was the successful candidate for the opposing solo position made available when Captain Andy Mackay finished his tour with the team that year. Captain Selby and Captain Chuck Mallett were practising the Co-Loop manoeuvre when a mid-air collision occurred at the top of the loop. Captain Mallett survived the collision. The Snowbirds dedicated the 2005 season to Captain Selby.

Captain Dave Boudreau *("Bood") First Line Astern 2005, Snowbird #4*

Captain Dave Boudreau ("Bood"), Snowbird #4

Captain Boudreau is from Dalhousie, New Brunswick. He joined the Canadian Forces in 1989 under the Officer Cadet Training Plan. After receiving his wings in 1991, he was posted to 407 Maritime Patrol Squadron in Comox, British Columbia, where he flew the CP-140 Aurora. In 1996, he was posted to 2 Canadian Forces Flying Training School in Moose Jaw, Saskatchewan, as a flying instructor on the CT-114 Tutor. Captain Boudreau subsequently made the transition to the CT-155 Hawk, one of the NATO Flying Training in Canada program's training aircraft.

Major Chris Hope ("Homer") Second Line Astern 2003/2004, Snowbird #5

Major Chris Hope ("Homer"), Snowbird #5, and Colonel Alain Boyer, Commander, 15 Wing Moose Jaw

Major Hope is from Blenheim, Ontario. He joined the Canadian Forces in 1986 under the Direct Entry Officer Program. After receiving his wings in 1988, he was posted to 2 Canadian Forces Flying Training School in Moose Jaw, Saskatchewan, as a flying instructor on the CT-114 Tutor. In 1992, he was posted to the Euro-NATO Joint Jet Pilot Training Program in Wichita Falls, Texas, where he instructed on the T-38 Talon. In 1995, Major Hope was posted to Central Flying School, as a CT-114 Tutor standards officer. In 2001, he was posted to 1 Canadian Air Division Headquarters with the responsibility for pilot training. Overall, Major Hope has accumulated over 2,200 instructional flying hours and achieved an A1 instructional rating.

Captain Andrew Mackay ("Droid") Outer Right Wing 2003, Snowbird #6; Opposing Solo 2004/2005, Snowbird #8

Captain Andy Mackay ("Droid"), Opposing Solo, with Major Todd Canterbury of the USAF Thunderbirds

Captain Mackay is from Orleans, Ontario. He joined the Canadian Forces in 1987 and, upon receiving his wings, was posted to Cold Lake, Alberta, as a rescue pilot on the Single Huey helicopter. In 1993, Captain Mackay was posted to 423 Maritime Helicopter Squadron in Shearwater, Nova Scotia, to fly the Sea King helicopter. Four years later, in 1997, he was posted to 2 Canadian Forces Flying Training School in Moose Jaw, Saskatchewan, as a flying instructor, where he attained an A2 instructional rating.

Captain Steve Chadwick ("Chappy") Outer Left Wing 2003/2004, Snowbird #7

Captain Steve Chadwick ("Chappy"), Snowbird #7

Captain Chadwick is from Hamilton, Ontario. He joined the Canadian Forces in 1992 under the Direct Entry Officer Program. After receiving his wings in 1997, Captain Chadwick went through fighter training and was subsequently posted to 433 Tactical Fighter Squadron in Bagotville, Quebec. While part of the 433 Squadron, Captain Chadwick successfully completed the Fighter Electronic Warfare and Radar and the Tactical Leadership Program flying courses. He also participated in two training and one operational deployment to Western Europe.

Patrick Gobeil's "Letter"

Explains Patrick: "I saw the Snowbirds for the first time in 1983. I was nine years old, attending a local air show in Bagotville, Quebec. I started collecting team brochures at that time. I got really interested in having my own Snowbirds' badge, which I remember seeing on the pilots' flying suits. Five years later I wrote a letter to 431 (Air Demonstration) Squadron, the Snowbirds, requesting the badge that I was looking for. Captain R. Lapointe wrote back to me, telling me that my request was impossible to fulfill since the badge is reserved for squadron members only. However, I kept the letter throughout my military career as a motivation source. On selection day, when I was told by the boss that he had a place for me on the team, I pulled the letter from my pocket and showed it to him. That was a very special day that I will never forget. I am extremely fortunate to be part of a team that continues to motivate and inspire Canadians throughout the country."

431 AIR DEMONSTRATION SQUADRON
CANADIAN FORCES BASE MOOSE JAW, BUSHELL PARK, SASKATCHEWAN SOH ONO TEL.(306) 694-2431
431e ESCADRON DE DÉMONSTRATION AÉRIENNE

1350-1 (431 esc)

21 April 1988

Patrick Gobeil
101 Ch. de la Savane
Ville de la baie, Québec
G7B 3N8

Cher Patrick;

Suite à ta lettre du 8 avril 88, qui demande l'escadron 431 de te donner un de nos écussons officiel, voici notre réponse.

Malheureusement, c'est la tradition de l'escadron de fournir l'écusson blanc et rouge aux membres de l'équipe seulement.

J'espère que tu viendras nous voir donner notre spectacle à la BFC Bagotville, le 18 et 19 juin 1988.

R. Lapointe
Capitaine

Captain Patrick Gobeil ("Gobble") Outer Right Wing 2004/2005, Snowbird #6

Captain Gobeil is from Ville de la Baie, Quebec. He graduated from the Centre Québécois de Formation Aéronautique in 1995, where he acquired a commercial license with multi-engine and instrument ratings. Enrolling in the Canadian Forces two years later, he received his wings in 2000 at Canadian Forces Base Portage la Prairie, Manitoba. In 2001, Captain Gobeil was transferred to Moose Jaw, Saskatchewan, as a flying instructor with 2 Canadian Forces Flying Training School.

Captain Patrick Gobeil ("Gobble"), Snowbird #6, and "the letter"

Captain Mike French ("Migs"), Snowbird #7, with Corporal Dan McIntyre

Captain Mike French *("Migs") Outer Left Wing 2005, Snowbird #7*

Captain French is from Langley, British Columbia. He joined the Canadian Forces in 1990 under the Regular Officer Training Plan and graduated from Royal Roads Military College with a degree in Computer Science and Space Science in 1994. After receiving his wings in 1995, he was posted to 2 Canadian Forces Flying Training School in Moose Jaw, Saskatchewan, as a flying instructor on the CT-114 Tutor. During his tour, he earned an A2 instructional rating and finished as a standards pilot.

In 2000, Captain French was selected for fighter-pilot training and was subsequently posted to 441 Tactical Fighter Squadron in Cold Lake, Alberta, where he flew the CF-18 Hornet. He participated in numerous NORAD and NATO exercises following the events of 11 September 2001.

Captain Wayne Mott ("Smut"), Snowbird #8, with his son, Nevada

Captain Wayne Mott *("Smut") Inner Right Wing 2001, Opposing Solo 2002, Lead Solo 2003, Snowbird #8*

Captain Mott is from Miramichi, New Brunswick. He joined the Canadian Forces in 1985 and was posted to 423 Squadron in Shearwater, Nova Scotia, to fly the Sea King helicopter. For six months in 1990, he flew the Twin Huey helicopter in support of the United Nations in Central America. In 1992, he was posted to 2 Canadian Forces Flying Training School in Moose Jaw, Saskatchewan, as a flying instructor, where he achieved an A2 instructional rating. In 1996, Captain Mott was posted to 443 Squadron in Victoria, British Columbia, to fly the Sea King helicopter. During this time, he completed two six-month tours in the Arabian Gulf, supporting United Nations' sanctions against Iraq.

Captain Chuck Mallett ("Chuck"), Lead Solo, with Master Corporal Darrell Fournier

Captain Chuck Mallett *("Chuck") Opposing Solo 2003, Lead Solo 2004/2005, Snowbird #9*

Captain Mallett is from Edmonton, Alberta. He joined the Canadian Forces in 1991 under the Officer Candidate Training Plan and graduated with a diploma in Aviation Science from Mount Royal College in Calgary, Alberta, in 1995. After receiving his wings in 1996, Captain Mallett was posted to 2 Canadian Forces Flying Training School in Moose Jaw, Saskatchewan, as a flying instructor on the CT-114 Tutor. In 1999, he was posted to the Flying Instructor's School in Moose Jaw and was subsequently selected for the initial cadre of instructors to help with the transition from the Tutor to the CT-156 Harvard II, the NATO Flying Training in Canada program's new training aircraft. Captain Mallett was posted to 431 (Air Demonstration) Squadron in 2002 as a standards pilot and as a member of the Snowbirds' home team.

First Woman Snowbird

One of the major milestones in military air demonstration history occurred in 2001, when Captain Maryse Carmichael made the team as Snowbird #3. Captain Carmichael was not only the first female pilot to make the team, but also the first female pilot to become a military jet demonstration-team pilot anywhere in the world. Captain Carmichael flew the 2002 season as Snowbird #2.

Captain Lyle Holbrook *Team Coordinator 2002/2003/2004, Snowbird #10*

Captain Holbrook is from Warwick, Ontario. He joined the Canadian Forces in 1990 through the Reserve Officer Pilot Training Program. He received his wings in 1992 and flew Kiowa helicopters, logging more than 1,000 hours at both 400 and 411 Squadrons. In 1996, Captain Holbrook followed 400 Squadron to 16 Wing Borden, where he flew the Griffon helicopter until being selected for the Snowbirds. While flying as a primary reservist, Captain Holbrook continued to work as a civilian pilot. He flew as a helicopter instructor pilot, a helicopter air ambulance pilot, out of Toronto, and a corporate jet pilot.

Captain Lyle Holbrook, Snowbird #10

Captain Tery Lebel *Team Coordinator 2005, Snowbird #10*

Captain Lebel is from Montreal, Quebec. He originally joined the Canadian Forces in 1974 as a trooper in the Armoured Corps (Reserve) and received a commission in 1975. In 1979, he transferred to the Air Force (Regular) and received his wings in 1981.

Captain Lebel's first tour was as an instructor pilot on the CT-114 Tutor aircraft in Moose Jaw, Saskatchewan. In 1986, he was posted to Tactical Helicopter Group where he flew CH-136 Kiowa, CH-135 Twin Huey, and CH-146 Griffon helicopters. He has been deployed on operations in Sinai, Somalia, and Haiti. In 2002, he was posted back to 15 Wing Moose Jaw as a flying instructor on the CT-156 Harvard II.

Captain Tery Lebel, Snowbird #10

Captain Claude Bertrand, Snowbird #11, (r),
with fellow coordinator Captain Lyle Holbrook

Captain Claude Bertrand *Team Coordinator 2003, Snowbird #11*

Captain Bertrand is from Alma, Quebec. He graduated in Engineering from McGill University in 1981. He worked as a professional engineer in the private sector and in the federal civil service for sixteen years prior to joining the Canadian Forces in 1997 under the Direct Entry Officer Program. He received his wings in 1998 and was selected to remain in Moose Jaw, Saskatchewan, as a flying instructor on the CT-114 Tutor and later on the CT-156 Harvard II.

Captain Gavin Crouch, Snowbird #11,
with Captain Stephanie Walker

Captain Gavin Crouch *Team Coordinator 2004/2005, Snowbird #11*

Captain Crouch is from Comox, British Columbia. He joined the military in 1993 under the Regular Officer Training Plan. After receiving his wings in 1998, he was posted to 440 (T) Squadron, Yellowknife, NWT, where he flew the CC-138 Twin Otter on floats, skis, and tundra tires. In 2001, he was posted to 2 Canadian Forces Flying Training School in Moose Jaw, Saskatchewan, as a flying instructor on the CT-156 Harvard II.

Longest Active Team Member

Marg Fowler has been with the Snowbirds since 1980 and is the only civilian member of the squadron. She is the operations support administrator and an integral part of the home team.

The 2003, 2004, and 2005 Teams

The 2003 Team

Major Steve Will	Snowbird 1 (Commanding Officer)
Captain Paul Couillard	Snowbird 2 (Inner Right Wing)
Captain Chris Bard	Snowbird 3 (Inner Left Wing)
Major Steve Melanson	Snowbird 4 (First Line Astern)
Major Chris Hope	Snowbird 5 (Second Line Astern)
Captain Andy Mackay	Snowbird 6 (Outer Right Wing)
Captain Steve Chadwick	Snowbird 7 (Outer Left Wing)
Captain Wayne Mott	Snowbird 8 (Lead Solo)
Captain Chuck Mallett	Snowbird 9 (Opposing Solo)
Captain Lyle Holbrook	Snowbird 10 (Team Coordinator)
Captain Claude Bertrand	Snowbird 11 (Team Coordinator)
Captain Stephanie Walker	Public Affairs Officer
Warrant Officer Dan Ross	Crew Chief (until July)
Sergeant Dave Scharf	Crew Chief (after July)
Master Corporal Jean-Marc Brien	Deputy Crew Chief
Master Corporal Rick Probetts	Lead Avionics Technician
Corporal Chris Rader-Martin	Lead Aviation Technician

Lt. General Fred Sutherland	Squadron Honorary Colonel
Major Stuart McIntosh	Deputy Commanding Officer
Captain Rick Thompson	Aircraft Maintenance Engineering Officer
Captain Dan Morrison	Squadron Logistics Officer
Captain Jayson Miles-Ingram	Standards Pilot
Mrs. Marg Fowler	Secretary
Master Warrant Officer Bob Brooks	Squadron Warrant Officer
Warrant Officer Joe Dierijck	Aircraft Technician
Sergeant Al Beasley	Aircraft Technician
Sergeant Grant Beeber	Supply Technician
Sergeant Luc Labrecque	Chief Clerk
Sergeant Mary Meier	Aircraft Technician
Sergeant Karen Waters	Aircraft Technician
Master Corporal Terry Allain	Aircraft Technician

Master Corporal Dwaine Barcier	Vehicle Technician
Master Corporal Tom Critchley	Aircraft Technician
Master Corporal Russ Davies	Aircraft Technician
Master Corporal Glen Duvall	Aircraft Technician
Master Corporal Sherry Duvall	Clerk
Master Corporal Anthony Forster	Aircraft Technician
Master Corporal Darrell Fournier	Aircraft Technician
Master Corporal Mike Grimard	Aircraft Technician
Master Corporal Dean Gullacher	Aircraft Technician
Master Corporal Brian Herde	Aircraft Technician
Master Corporal Tammy Kohorst	Aircraft Technician
Master Corporal Shawn Stone	Aircraft Technician
Master Corporal Sheldon Stotz	Aircraft Technician
Master Corporal Michael Underwood	Aircraft Technician
Corporal Mark Benham	Aircraft Technician
Corporal Jean-Pierre Bérubé	Aircraft Technician
Corporal Joel Charron	Aircraft Technician
Corporal Alvin Cole	Aircraft Technician
Corporal Karen Dierijck	Aircraft Technician
Corporal Greg Folliott	Aircraft Technician
Corporal Daniel Gray	Aircraft Technician
Corporal Micky Kelly	Aircraft Technician
Corporal Robert Kilbride	Aircraft Technician
Corporal Patrick Marceau	Aircraft Technician
Corporal Daniel McIntyre	Aircraft Technician
Corporal Ian McIvor	Aircraft Technician
Corporal Terry McLaren	Supply Technician
Corporal Eric Molsan	Aircraft Technician
Corporal Robert Muise	Aircraft Technician
Corporal Michael Pelletier	Aircraft Technician
Corporal Robert Oddy	Aircraft Technician
Corporal Robert O'Reilly	Aircraft Technician
Corporal Brian Phillips	Aircraft Technician
Corporal Richard Pilon	Aircraft Technician
Corporal Ian Rensby	Aircraft Technician

Corporal Ron Roy	Aircraft Technician
Corporal Kamaljit Singh	Aircraft Technician
Corporal Dave Talbot	Aircraft Technician
Corporal Kendall Tobin	Supply Technician
Corporal Laurie Walsh	Supply Technician
Corporal Ryan Willett	Aircraft Technician
Corporal Rick Yuke	Aircraft Technician
Private Zack Crawshaw	Aircraft Technician
Private Matt Faulkner	Aircraft Technician
Private Christian Lentz	Aircraft Technician
Private Jennifer Lyons	Clerk

The 2004 Team

Major Steve Will	Snowbird 1 (Commanding Officer/Team Lead)
Captain Paul Couillard	Snowbird 2 (Inner Right Wing)
Captain Cory Blakely	Snowbird 3 (Inner Left Wing)
Captain Miles Selby	Snowbird 4 (First Line Astern)
Major Chris Hope	Snowbird 5 (Second Line Astern)
Captain Patrick Gobeil	Snowbird 6 (Outer Right Wing)
Captain Steve Chadwick	Snowbird 7 (Outer Left Wing)
Captain Andrew Mackay	Snowbird 8 (Opposing Solo)
Captain Chuck Mallett	Snowbird 9 (Lead Solo)
Captain Lyle Holbrook	Snowbird 10 (Team Coordinator)
Captain Gavin Crouch	Snowbird 11 (Team Coordinator)
Captain Stephanie Walker	Public Affairs Officer
Sergeant Dave Scharf	Crew Chief
Master Corporal Darrell Fournier	Deputy Crew Chief
Corporal David Talbot	Lead Avionics Technician
Corporal Ryan Willett	Lead Aviation Technician

Lt. General Fred Sutherland	Squadron Honorary Colonel
Major Stuart McIntosh	Deputy Commanding Officer
Lt. Commander Mike Brown	Chaplain
Major Pierre Morissette	Flight Surgeon
Captain Sandra Holloway	Squadron Logistics Officer

Captain Hugo Pellerin	Aircraft Maintenance Engineering Officer
Captain Jayson Miles-Ingram	Standards and Training Officer
Captain Rob Reichert	Standards and Training Officer
Master Warrant Officer Doug Stone	Squadron Warrant Officer
Mrs. Marg Fowler	Secretary
Warrant Officer Jim Flach	Aircraft Repair Officer
Warrant Officer Tony Pettipas	Aircraft Control Officer
Sergeant Grant Beeber	Supply Technician
Sergeant Alain Croussette	Aviation Technician
Sergeant Herbert Heidt	Aircraft Structures Technician
Sergeant Luc Labrecque	Chief Clerk
Sergeant Mary Meier	Aviation Technician
Sergeant Barry Ripley	Aviation Technician
Sergeant Karen Waters	Aviation Technician
Master Corporal Terry Allain	Aviation Technician
Master Corporal Dwaine Barcier	Vehicle Technician
Master Corporal Jean-Marc Brien	Aviation Technician
Master Corporal Tom Critchley	Aircraft Structures Technician
Master Corporal Russ Davies	Aircraft Structures Technician
Master Corporal Glen Duvall	Aviation Technician
Master Corporal Sherry Duvall	Clerk
Master Corporal Tony Forster	Avionics Technician
Master Corporal Mike Grimard	Aviation Technician
Master Corporal Dean Gullacher	Avionics Technician
Master Corporal Brian Herde	Aviation Technician
Master Corporal Tammy Kohorst	Aviation Technician
Master Corporal Rick Probetts	Avionics Technician
Master Corporal Shawn Stone	Aviation Technician
Master Corporal Sheldon Stotz	Non-Destructive Testing Technician
Master Corporal Michael Underwood	Aviation Technician
Corporal Marc Belhumeur	Aviation Technician
Corporal Jean-Pierre Bérubé	Aviation Technician
Corporal Daniel Gray	Aircraft Structures Technician
Corporal Ken Hall	Aircraft Structures Technician
Corporal Nick Katuski	Aviation Technician

Corporal Micky Kelly	Avionics Technician
Corporal Robert Kilbride	Aviation Technician
Corporal Jennifer Lyons	Clerk
Corporal Daniel McIntyre	Aviation Technician
Corporal Ian McIvor	Aircraft Structures Technician
Corporal Terry McLaren	Supply Technician
Corporal Eric Moisan	Aviation Technician
Corporal Shawn Murphy	Aviation Technician
Corporal Tracy Nicholas	Aviation Technician
Corporal Robert Oddy	Avionics Technician
Corporal Bob O'Reilly	Avionics Technician
Corporal Guy Palin	Aviation Technician
Corporal Brian Phillips	Aviation Technician
Corporal Richard Pilon	Aviation Technician
Corporal Chris Rader-Martin	Aviation Technician
Corporal Andrew Rees	Avionics Technician
Corporal Ian Rensby	Avionics Technician
Corporal Mirko Robertson	Aviation Technician
Corporal Ron Roy	Aviation Technician
Corporal Cameron Simms	Avionics Technician
Corporal Kevin Spooner	Aviation Technician
Corporal Kendall Tobin	Supply Technician
Corporal Laurie Walsh	Supply Technician
Corporal Rick Yuke	Aviation Technician
Private Matt Faulkner	Aviation Technician
Private Christian Lentz	Aviation Technician

The 2005 Team

Major Ian McLean	Snowbird 1 (Commanding Officer/Team Lead)
Captain Paul Couillard	Snowbird 2 (Inner Right Wing)
Major Cory Blakely	Snowbird 3 (Inner Left Wing)
Captain David Boudreau	Snowbird 4 (First Line Astern)
Major Chris Hope	Snowbird 5 (Second Line Astern)
Captain Patrick Gobeil	Snowbird 6 (Outer Right Wing)
Captain Mike French	Snowbird 7 (Outer Left Wing)

Captain Andrew Mackay	Snowbird 8 (Opposing Solo)
Captain Chuck Mallett	Snowbird 9 (Lead Solo)
Captain Tery Lebel	Snowbird 10 (Team Coordinator)
Captain Gavin Crouch	Snowbird 11 (Team Coordinator)
Captain Stephanie Walker	Public Affairs Officer (until June)
Lieutenant (Navy) Petra Smith	Public Affairs Officer (after June)
Sergeant Dave Scharf	Crew Chief
Master Corporal Darrell Fournier	Deputy Crew Chief
Master Corporal Tony Forster	Lead Avionics Technician
Corporal Tracy Nicholas	Lead Aviation Technician
Lt. General Fred Sutherland	Squadron Honorary Colonel
Major Stuart McIntosh	Deputy Commanding Officer
Lt. Commander Mike Brown	Chaplain
Major Pierre Morissette	Flight Surgeon
Captain Colin Cragg	Operations Support Officer
Captain Ian James	Standards and Training Officer
Captain Hugo Pellerin	Aircraft Maintenance Engineering Officer
Master Warrant Officer Doug Stone	Squadron Warrant Officer
Mrs. Marg Fowler	Secretary
Warrant Officer Jim Flach	Aircraft Repair Officer
Warrant Officer Mike Overs	Avionics Technician
Sergeant George Abbott	Aircraft Structures Technician
Sergeant Grant Beeber	Supply Technician
Sergeant Alain Croussette	Aviation Technician
Sergeant Luc Labrecque	Chief Clerk
Sergeant Mary Meier	Aviation Technician
Sergeant Barry Ripley	Avionics Technician
Sergeant Maxwell Tibbo	Traffic Technician
Sergeant Karen Waters	Aviation Technician
Master Corporal Terry Allain	Avionics Technician
Master Corporal Dwaine Barcier	Vehicle Technician
Master Corporal Jean-Marc Brien	Aviation Technician
Master Corporal Grant Forness	Avionics Technician
Master Corporal Ken Hall	Aircraft Structures Technician

Master Corporal Herbert Heidt	Aircraft Structures Technician
Master Corporal Brian Herde	Aviation Technician
Master Corporal Tammy Kohorst	Aviation Technician
Master Corporal Sandra Overs	Avionics Technician
Master Corporal Rick Probetts	Avionics Technician
Master Corporal Shawn Stone	Aviation Technician
Master Corporal Sheldon Stotz	Non-destructive Testing Technician
Master Corporal Michael Underwood	Aviation Technician
Corporal Claude Aucoin	Aircraft Structures Technician
Corporal Marc Belhumeur	Aviation Technician
Corporal Jean-Pierre Bérubé	Aviation Technician
Corporal Tim Collis	Aviation Technician
Corporal Matt Faulkner	Aviation Technician
Corporal Daniel Gray	Aircraft Structures Technician
Corporal Bill Harley	Supply Technician
Corporal Nick Katuski	Avionics Technician
Corporal Micky Kelly	Avionics Technician
Corporal Robert Kilbride	Aviation Technician
Corporal Christian Lentz	Aviation Technician
Corporal Jennifer Lyons	Deputy Chief Clerk
Corporal Dave MacDonald	Telecommunications Information Specialist
Corporal Daniel McIntyre	Aviation Technician
Corporal Ben Miron	Aircraft Structures Technician
Corporal Eric Moisan	Aviation Technician
Corporal Shawn Murphy	Aviation Technician
Corporal Bob O'Reilly	Avionics Technician
Corporal Robert Oddy	Avionics Technician
Corporal Guy Palin	Aviation Technician
Corporal Robert Parker	Aviation Technician
Corporal Brian Phillips	Aviation Technician
Corporal John Pietrzak	Aviation Technician
Corporal Richard Pilon	Aviation Technician
Corporal Fred Racz	Aviation Technician
Corporal Andrew Rees	Aviation Technician
Corporal Ian Rensby	Avionics Technician

Corporal Garry Richards	Aviation Technician
Corporal Mirko Robertson	Aviation Technician
Corporal Christian Roy	Aviation Technician
Corporal Ron Roy	Aviation Technician
Corporal Cameron Simms	Avionics Technician
Corporal Ian Slater	Aircraft Structures Technician
Corporal Kevin Spooner	Aviation Technician
Corporal Dave Talbot	Avionics Technician
Corporal Laurie Walsh	Supply Technician
Corporal Ryan Willett	Aviation Technician
Corporal Rick Yuke	Aviation Technician
Private Matt Travis	Supply Technician

Other Military Aerobatic Demonstration Teams

There are twenty military aerobatic-demonstration teams, in addition to the Snowbirds, operating in the world today. They not only represent some of the world's major powers, but also some countries one might not expect to host such a team. The current teams and the aircraft they fly are:

Biele Albatrosy (Slovakia)	L-39 Albatross (Aero Vodochody)
Black Knights (Singapore)	Super Skyhawk A4SU (4), F-16 (2)
Blue Angels (United States, Navy)	F/A-18 Hornet (Boeing)
Blue Impulse (Japan)	T-4 (Kawasaki)
Esquadriha da Fumaca (Brazil)	EMB-312 Tucano (Embraer)
Il Freece Tricolori (Italy)	Aermacchi MB339PAN
The Halcones (Chile)	Extra 300S (Walter)
La Patrouille (France)	Alpha Jet
Marche Verte (Morocco)	CAP 231
Patrouille Suisse (Switzerland)	F-5E Tiger II (Northrop)
Patrulla Aguila (Spain)	CASA C.101AG Aviojet
Royal Jordanian Falcons (Jordan)	Extra 300S (Walter)
Russian Knights (Russia)	Su-27 Flanker/Su-35 Flanker Plus
Team 60 (Sweden)	Sk.60 (Saab)
Team Iskry (Poland)	TS-11 Iskra
The Red Arrows (United Kingdom)	Hawk (BAE)

The Roulettes (Australia)	PC-9 Turbotrainer (Pilatus)
Thunderbirds (United States, Air Force)	F-16 Fighting Falcon (Lockheed)
Turkish Stars (Turkey)	NF-5A Freedom Fighter
Ukrainian Falcons (Ukraine)	MiG-29 "Fulcrum"

The USAF Thunderbirds in formation

In North America, three aerobatic demonstration teams perform each year: the Snowbirds, the United States Air Force Thunderbirds, and the United States Navy Blue Angels.

The Thunderbirds are based at Nellis Air Force Base in Nevada. They fly the F-16 Fighting Falcon and proudly represent the United States Air Force. The full team numbers approximately 120 members. The show team is made up of six pilots and planes: Team Lead, Left Wing, Right Wing, Slot, Lead Solo, and Opposing Solo.

The U.S. Navy Blue Angels call Pensacola, Florida, home. They fly F/A-18s, with their familiar blue and yellow colours. They also perform a six-plane show. Not only are they supported by a top-notch ground crew, but the Blue Angels' transport is also part of the performance. The Marine Corps C-130 Hercules Transport (known as Fat Albert) puts on quite a show with its Jet Assisted Take-Off.

The Dayton 2003 air show was a real treat—all three North American teams performed at that show, which is a rare event. When teams get together on the road, it's a chance for them to catch up, talk shop, exchange ride-alongs, and socialize.

U.S. Navy Blue Angels #5 and #6 mirror each other as they perform a "Dirty Pass."

The West Coast Demo CF-18—A Bonus

During the 2003 season, I had the pleasure of seeing and photographing one of the most-recognized military aircraft in the world—the West Coast Demo CF-18, piloted by Captain Travis Brassington from 410 "Cougar" Squadron at 4 Wing Cold Lake, Alberta. This jet sports one of the finest paint jobs ever seen on a military aircraft. Cold Lake artist Jim Belliveau is responsible for the design, which was painted onto the jet to promote the Tiger Meet of the Americas. Tiger meets are military flying competitions in which all of the participants are from squadrons represented by "big cats," such as tigers and cougars.

Captain Travis Brassington and the Demo CF-18 in a "Full Burner" takeoff.

Representing future Snowbirds, from left to right, are
Mackenzie Scharf, Sydney Scharf, Brendan Hope, and Jeremy Hope

About the Photographer

Earning the Snowbirds' trust and being welcomed into their "family" to observe and record their truly unique story from the inside is every photographer's dream. Shooting from the cockpit at high speed while flying upside down and "pulling Gs" puts a whole new meaning into the words "action photography." It's a wonderful story and I feel privileged to be the one to tell it. This book is truly a "project of a lifetime."

—Mike Sroka
www.mikesroka.com

Mike Sroka is a highly respected and creative commercial photographer, originally from the Chicago area, now living and working in Canada. For more than twenty years, he has produced striking photographs for clients such as Carewest, Bolens, Husky Oil, NOVA, Parks Canada, Harley-Davidson, Miller Beer, Firestone, Wrangler, and Diet Pepsi. Sroka's portfolios of outstanding images taken at fast-paced Indy Car and Formula One races, and at the Calgary Exhibition and Stampede, have proven his exceptional skill as a high-energy, action photographer.